Aging in Chinese Society:
A Holistic Approach
to the Experience of Aging
in Taiwan and Singapore

Aging in Chinese Society: A Holistic Approach to the Experience of Aging in Taiwan and Singapore

Homer L. Jernigan, PhD, MDiv
Margaret B. Jernigan, MEd, RN, MIS, MS

℈℟℔℔

The Haworth Pastoral Press
An Imprint of The Haworth Press, Inc.
New York • London • Norwood (Australia)

Published by

The Haworth Pastoral Press, Inc., 10 Alice Street, Binghamton, NY 13904-1580 USA

The Haworth Pastoral Press is an Imprint of The Haworth Press, Inc., 10 Alice Street, Binghamton, NY 13904-1580 USA.

Aging in Chinese Society: A Holistic Approach to the Experience of Aging in Taiwan and Singapore has also been published as the *Journal of Religious Gerontology,* Volume 8, Number 3 1992.

Library of Congress Cataloging-in-Publication Data

Jernigan, Homer L.
Aging in Chinese society : a holistic approach to the experience of aging in Taiwan and Singapore / Homer L. Jernigan, Margaret B. Jernigan.
    p. cm.
Also published as: Journal of religious gerontology, vol. 8, no. 3, 1992.
Includes bibliographical references and index.
ISBN 1-56024-273-6 (alk. paper)
    1. Aged—Taiwan—Social conditions. 2. Aged—Singapore—Social conditions. 3. Aging—Social aspects—Taiwan. 4. Aging—Social aspects—Singapore. I. Jernigan, Margaret B. II. Title.
HQ1064.T28J47 1992
305.26'095124'9—dc20
                                                                        92-13222
                                                                            CIP

Aging in Chinese Society:
A Holistic Approach
to the Experience of Aging
in Taiwan and Singapore

Aging in Chinese Society: A Holistic Approach to the Experience of Aging in Taiwan and Singapore

CONTENTS

Preface   xi

Acknowledgments   xiii

Chapter One: Introduction   1

Chapter Two: A Brief Introduction to Taiwan and Singapore   9

Chapter Three: Aging in Traditional Chinese Society   19

Chapter Four: Two Rapidly Changing Chinese Societies   27

Chapter Five: Aging in Rapidly Changing Chinese Societies: A Summary and Interpretation of Our Study   33

Chapter Six: Individual Responses to a Changing Chinese Society (Taiwan)   59

Chapter Seven: Interactions of Personality, Culture, and Religion in the Experience of Aging   73

Chapter Eight: Implications and Conclusions   95

References   105

Appendix A: Experts and Official Informants Interviewed in Taiwan and Singapore   109

Appendix B: Interviews with Elders: Guidelines Provided to Students (1989)   111

Index   117

ABOUT THE AUTHORS

Homer L. Jernigan, PhD, MDiv, was Albert V. Danielsen Professor of Pastoral Care and Counseling at Boston University School of Theology where he taught for thirty-three years. He has had experience as a parish minister and hospital chaplain. Dr. Jernigan's current interest is the problems and opportunities of the elderly in various cultural and religious contexts. He is a member of the American Psychological Association and the Society for Pastoral Theology, and a Diplomate of the American Association of Pastoral Counselors.

Margaret B. Jernigan, MEd, RN, MIS, MS, is Assistant Professor of Nursing in the Department of Nursing at Simmons College. She also consults and teaches ethical issues in health care. Ms. Jernigan is a member of the American Nurses Association, the American Public Health Association, The Hastings Center, the Massachusetts Nurses Association Cabinet on Ethics, and the Society for Health and Human Values.

Preface

An opportunity to live and work in Singapore for seven months in 1991 and to spend some time in Taiwan gave us a chance to reflect on the relevance of what is written here. What we have written is based on research that we did in Taiwan and Singapore in 1985. We had done various kinds of preparation before 1985, and we have supplemented our report with some more recent data. During our time in Singapore and Taiwan in 1991, however, we wondered how relevant what we had written earlier was to the situation of Chinese elders in the 1990s.

We did not go to Singapore and Taiwan in 1991 for the specific purpose of continuing our research in the experience of aging. We did, however, have opportunities to observe Chinese families with elderly members, to talk with some people who were knowledgeable about aging, to read information that was printed in the daily press and in government publications, and to talk with some church groups about the situation of the aging.

As we reflect on what we had written earlier in the light of what we learned in 1991, we feel that the issues that we raised then continue to be important. Six years after our original research, we see even more clearly that the experience of aging involves adjustment to many changes and losses. We see the importance of what we said earlier concerning the problems for elders and their families which are associated with catastrophic and chronic illness. We see some of the things that happen as the elderly become increasingly dependent on other family members. We see continuing changes in family life as the younger generation grows up and leaves home, and even leaves the country. We see changes in family patterns and values as the standard of living continues to rise. We see changes in peer relationships among elders as peers become physically more limited, move away, or die. We see continuing changes in the roles, status, and functions of Chinese elders; and we wonder about the sources of meaning and purpose in their lives, as we did in 1985. We see even more clearly the importance of what we have called in our report (Chapter Seven) the "spiritual" aspects of life that help the elderly to adjust to and transcend the changes and losses that they experience. And, as we observe what is happening in the Chinese societies of Taiwan and Singapore, especially, changes in the relationships between the generations, we wonder about the traditional Chinese values which have been so important in the experience of aging in these societies. How much longer will the traditional values of filial piety, reciprocity between the generations, and respect for elders continue to undergird the possibility of a "good life" for the older members of Chinese families?

As we reflect on such observations, we are aware of the importance of studies that can follow-up the kind of research we did in 1985 and make note of the changes through the years that affect the lives of people like the ones we interviewed. And we are aware that, as changes in lifestyle and health care make possible more years of physical survival, there is increasing need for attention to those things that influence the quality of life for older people in the various phases and stages of the aging process. We are particularly concerned about what we see happening to Chinese elders in the context of their rapidly changing societies; but we are aware that similar things are happening to the elderly in many other cultures around the world.

Margaret B. and Homer L. Jernigan
September, 1991

Acknowledgments

We acknowledge with gratitude the support of the Marion and Jasper Whiting Foundation, which made our research in Taiwan and Singapore possible. We owe much to friends in Taiwan and Singapore who helped us in making arrangements for our interviews and assisted us in coping with a difficult situation that we experienced in Singapore. We learned much from the teachers, researchers, and officials in both countries who gave of their time and expertise. We are particularly grateful to the elders who responded so graciously to our requests to talk with them. The one person who contributed the most to our work in Taiwan was our research assistant, Kuan Jyn Li, and we acknowledge the many ways in which she befriended us and supported our efforts.

Chapter One

Introduction

Since the early 1970s, we, the joint authors, have been interested in Chinese society. In 1971-72, we spent a sabbatical year in Singapore with our family. We engaged in a variety of activities, and our research interest was the response to death in traditional Chinese society. We learned much about Chinese culture, particularly the Chinese family system and the meaning and significance of Chinese mourning and burial customs. The results of our research were published privately, but also publicly, in two abridged versions (Jernigan, 1973, 1986).

After our return from Singapore, we continued to pursue our general interests in pastoral care and community health, but we became increasingly concerned with the problems of the elderly. Homer began teaching courses in ethnicity and aging as part of his regular teaching load, and Margaret included work with elderly patients and lectures on aging in her teaching.

In 1985, a grant from the Whiting Foundation in Boston made it possible for us to do research on aging in Chinese society. We visited both Taiwan and Singapore in the summer of that year. We were interested in going to Taiwan because of the continuities with the traditional Chinese culture that we had studied in our first visit to Singapore. We wanted to know what had happened to family life, particularly to the older members of the family, under the changing conditions in Taiwan. We were interested in going to Singapore because of our previous experience there and our impression that the same processes of modernization, urbanization, and industrialization that were taking place in Taiwan had been going on in Singapore for a longer period of time. We knew that both countries had been engaged for some time in economic and political development that made it possible for them to compete successfully in world markets.

In Taiwan we were able, with the aid of an interpreter, to conduct interviews with twenty-four Chinese elders and ten resource persons who were knowledgeable concerning the situation of the aging in Taiwan. We also had access to reports of studies of aging in a farming village (Hsieh, 1984) and a fishing village (Chuan, 1984) and earlier studies of farm and village life by Virginia Wolf (1968, 1972). We supplemented our Taiwan interviews with data and recommendations from two reports on the elderly in Singapore–the *Report on the National Survey of Senior Citizens* sponsored by the Ministry of Social Affairs (1983), and the *Report of the Committee on the Problems of the Aged*, sponsored by the Ministry of Health (1984). We had access to some other literature, including an unpublished study of Chinese elders in Kreta Ayer, the old "Chinatown," section of Singapore (Wong, 1982), and we were able to interview a few resource persons. A reader in Singapore who read the first draft of this report helped us to update some of the information about Singapore and the situation of the elderly in that country (Wee, 1987). A list of the resource persons who were interviewed in Taiwan and Singapore is provided in Appendix A and the relevant literature is listed in the "References."

SOME ASSUMPTIONS

In our teaching, we are both concerned about understanding and working with " whole persons in their whole environment." For Margaret, this involves teaching community health nursing; for Homer, pastoral care in congregation and community. For our teaching and research we are concerned about a holistic approach to the experience of persons. We recognize that a holistic approach needs to include the "religious" or "spiritual" aspects of experience. Without using the words "religious" or "spiritual," we have tried to include important aspects of what we understand those words to mean in the development of a theoretical framework by which to relate the interactions of individual persons and their cultural environment. Our efforts to develop a holistic perspective on the experience of aging include four basic aspects of what we think it means to be a ''person'':

- the physical survival aspects, which have to do with a person's ability to cope with the necessities of human existence (food, clothing, shelter, income, health, sanitation, mobility, sleep, exercise, etc.);
- the relational (social-emotional) aspects, which have to do with a person's ability to relate to other persons (one-to-one, family, peer group, and various forms of social and communal relationships) not only for coping but also for various forms of emotional satisfaction including ''love'';
- the validation aspects, which have to do with a person's sense of worth or self-esteem, or in Asian terms, the sense of ''place'' or ''face'' in the family, community, and world;
- the self and world transcendence aspects, which have to do with a person's sense of the meaning and purpose of life and the life commitments and relationships that facilitate adjustment to and transcendence of the day-to-day vicissitudes of life.

From a holistic perspective, these four aspects of personal experience interact with each other. They are four different ways of looking at the total experience of an individual person, and they are not separate and distinct categories of experience. We are indebted to a variety of sources for our understanding of these four aspects of personal experience, particularly to the writings of Carl Rogers (1951), William Glasser (1965), and Abraham Maslow (1968).

We are interested in the interactions of personality and culture in the experience of aging, and these four aspects of personal experience help us to identify and study ways in which a particular culture:

- develops access to natural resources, information, tools, technologies, coping patterns, institutions, and systems that contribute to the survival of the individual and the culture;

- provides mutually supportive and need-satisfying forms of social interaction (socialization);
- defines the status, role, and functions of the individual in the light of the culture's values and priorities and enables the individual to experience a sense of personal worth and significance;
- develops collective sources of meaning and purpose for life in which individuals can participate and that, to some extent, they can internalize through participation in the myths, symbols, and rituals of the culture and/or some form of its religious heritage.

We understand that the interactions of any particular individual with his or her culture is always unique, and any effort to look at the interactions of a particular ethnic group with their culture risks losing the richness of individual experience. For our study, we were interested in reporting both the uniqueness of the experience of individuals we interviewed and some general impressions of the experience of aging in the Chinese societies of Taiwan and Singapore; but we recognized the difficulties of the task.

With the time and resources available to us, a reliable quantitative survey of the elderly in Taiwan and Singapore was not possible. We used a modified "phenomenological" approach, supplemented by reading in relevant literature and interviews with resource persons. We wanted to learn as much as we could about the experience of aging from the perspective of persons involved in that process, and we kept this goal in mind in the interviews we conducted with Chinese elders. Out of previous studies of persons of various ages and different ethnic backgrounds, we had developed our four categories or "themes" for collecting data about each person's experience of aging. Ideally, we wanted to be able to participate empathically in each person's unique situation and to understand as much as we could about what it was like for him or her to be in that situation. The specifics of the data collected were not as important as our efforts to understand how each person, in the context of his or her struggle to cope with the realities of life and to relate to other people, was able to put life together and to find a sense of personal worth and a meaning and purpose for life. Our reading was important to help us to understand the cultural context in which each person was going through the experience of aging. Our interviews with our resource persons were important to give us a sense of the actual and potential cultural resources that were available to the elders we interviewed and to the age mates in their society.

LIMITATIONS

There were, of course, important limitations on what we tried to do in Taiwan and Singapore. Our interview sample was limited to two cities in Taiwan and, then, to the twenty-four elders whom we were able to contact through the sources that were available to us. We were fortunate in the diversity which was included in such a "convenience" sample. There were eleven women and thirteen men. Sixteen were Taiwanese (Chinese born in Taiwan) and eight were "Mainlanders" (born in Mainland China and emigrating to Taiwan in 1948 or later). Five had little or no formal education, six had secondary school, twelve had various amounts of college education, and one had a graduate degree. They were mostly "middle class," but four were farm or working class, and three were "upper class." Their present or past occupations included six school personnel (teachers or administrators), five shopkeepers, four homemakers, three self-employed, two government workers, two artists, one nurse, and one pharmacist. Eleven considered themselves "retired." Eleven were currently involved in some kind of volunteer activity outside the home. The age range was from 55 to 81. Thirteen were between 60 and 69, eight were between 70 and 79, two were between 55 and 60, and one was 81. Of those who identified their religion, seven were nominal or active Buddhists, four were Christian, two were humanists in the Confucian tradition, and five had "no religion."

The interviews were conducted in their homes, the shops where they worked, or the activity centers where they were serving as volunteers or participating in the activity programs. There were limitations on the amount of time that we could spend with each person. We could have only one interview with each person, but we felt we were able to ask the questions we needed to ask in each interview. The most obvious limitation was language. Neither of us spoke or understood Mandarin or Taiwanese (the two Chinese dialects most common in Taiwan). We were fortunate to have an interpreter who was fluent in Mandarin, Taiwanese, and English. She was an attractive young person who quickly established rapport with the interviewees, and we were amazed at how readily most persons answered our questions and how few problems the language barrier posed. Most of the people with whom we spoke seemed to enjoy talking with us, and we enjoyed talking with them. We had made some efforts, working with our interpreter, to develop ways of asking questions that would communicate with the elders we were interviewing. The questions were adaptations of ones that had been previously developed for the use of students interviewing elders in ethnic groups in the Boston area. A revised form of the interview guide for current students at Boston University is included in Appendix B.

For practical reasons, we were not able to interview elders in Singapore. We interviewed a few resource persons to supplement our previous knowledge of the situation of the aging in Singapore, and we received copies of the two government reports mentioned earlier. The National Survey of Senior Citizens had been conducted under the auspices of the Ministry of Social Affairs in 1982, and the results were published in 1983. The Survey was based on a sample of 5,538 persons. The sample had approximately the same composition in terms of sex, age, ethnicity, and marital status as the general population fifty-five and above in Singapore (245,016 persons). Eighty-one percent of the respondents were Chinese, and seventy-two percent were age sixty and above. Since retirement age in Singapore at that time was fifty-five, the results of the study were skewed toward the younger age groups (52% of the sample was under 65, and 71% under 70). The aging population in Singapore is growing and changing rapidly, just as the aging population is in other countries, and the data of a survey conducted in 1982 need to be interpreted with caution. We used the data of the report as a quantitative check on our more qualitative data from Taiwan, assuming that there were similarities in the cultural situations of Taiwan and Singapore because of the rapid development of technology, urbanization, and industrialization. These two countries share a common Chinese background with the largest ethnic group in both countries being from the same part of China. The *Report of the Committee on the Problems of the Aged* (1984) was also somewhat out of date, but it was of interest as it identified problems affecting the experience of aging in Singapore, evaluated existing resources, and made recommendations concerning the development of new approaches to the identified problems. We saw many similar problems in Taiwan.

In our report, we will not attempt to summarize the data and impressions that we have collected from Taiwan and Singapore in detail. We want to provide some background material on both countries and to summarize some of the important aspects of aging in traditional Chinese society. We will then describe some of the important social and cultural developments that are contributing to changes in the experience of aging in Taiwan and Singapore and will summarize some of the things that we have learned about the interactions of personality and culture in response to these changes. We will use our "holistic" approach to the interactions of personality and culture to organize and interpret what we have learned from our reading and our interviews, with a special emphasis on what we see as the "religious" or "spiritual" aspects of such an approach. Our general impressions, based on our interviews, will be supplemented with a sample of individual "stories" that were shared with us by our interviewees.

Chapter Two

A Brief Introduction
to Taiwan and Singapore

The context in which an experience takes place influences the nature and meaning of that experience in many ways. Although we were primarily interested in the influence of ethnicity on the experience of aging, we recognized that ethnicity cannot be separated from other aspects of the cultural context. There were many things that we needed to know about Taiwan and Singapore in order to understand what we saw, heard, and read. The data about things like geography, history, politics, economics, education, and religion were important and helped us to get the "feel" of what it was like to live there; but there are always less tangible aspects of the "feel" of a place that cannot be captured by facts and figures. In some ways, our experience of living in Singapore for a year was the best way to gain some appreciation of the context of Chinese culture, particularly when we were doing so much listening and reading concerning traditional Chinese culture as well as contemporary life in Singapore. Our continuing contacts with Chinese friends and students from Singapore since 1972 and our more recent visits there have also helped. However, there are important differences in Taiwanese and Singaporean contexts for the experience of aging that are reflected in data about different aspects of life in these two countries.

TAIWAN

Taiwan is an island located about 120 miles from the mainland China province of Fukien, now known as Fujian (the data in this section, unless otherwise noted, come from Reid, 1984). Taiwan is 220 miles north of the Philippine island of Luzon and 370 miles southwest of Okinawa. The island straddles the Tropic of Cancer, which means that the north has a sub-tropical climate while the south has a tropical climate. The island is about 250 miles long and 80 miles wide at its broadest point. It is shaped something like a tobacco leaf, with its tip pointing toward Japan. There is a mountain range that runs from north to south, covering much of Eastern and Central Taiwan. Sixty-two peaks rise to more than 10,000 feet above sea level, and much of the mountainous area is eight to ten thousand feet high. The east coast has a narrow plain that rises to high cliffs along the Pacific Ocean. Most of the people live in the cities on the plains west of the mountains. These plains have some of the richest soil in that part of the world and have been under intensive farming for centuries. Rice is the primary crop, but sugar cane and a wide variety of fruits and vegetables are also grown. There are large tea plantations in the mountains. Taiwan has been a major exporter of farm and forest products (particularly camphor) since the nineteenth century. An average of forty inches of rainfall per year (more in higher elevations) makes for abundant moisture and a very humid climate all year round.

The most important fact of Taiwan's modern history was the coming of the Nationalist (Kuomintang) Chinese army and Chiang Kai-Shek's followers from Mainland China in 1949. The increasingly precarious position of the Nationalists after four years of civil war on the Mainland led to the exodus. Taiwan had been returned to China at the end of World War II, after fifty years of Japanese occupation. The Nationalists were, thus, withdrawing to a Chinese province from which they hoped to return to the Mainland and to rule all of China once more. The return to the Mainland did not materialize, and Chiang Kai-Shek and his followers, while maintaining a strong military presence, continued the modernization of Taiwan that the Japanese had begun. A massive land reform program took the farms from the rich landlords and made it possible for small farmers to own their own land. At the same time, the landlords were reimbursed for their property and given incentives to invest in industry. A rapid industrial revolution followed, involving government-business cooperation in developing industries and finding world markets for Taiwanese products. Within thirty years, a country that had been primarily rural and agricultural became primarily urban and industrial. But the farmers were not forgotten, and two of the early efforts were the electrification of the rural areas and the improvement of transportation. Educational reforms made education available to all children and encouraged advanced study in Taiwan and abroad in the fields that were needed for a modern technological society. The per capita income and the standard of living in terms of housing, food, education, and consumer consumption rose rapidly. The people of Taiwan responded to the efforts of the government with their own initiative, ingenuity, and industriousness to compete successfully in the modern world. The population of Taiwan also increased dramatically after 1949; but the language and ethnic divisions between Taiwanese and Mainlanders have not disappeared. Many Mainlanders experienced painful separations from their families of origin and were not allowed to visit them or to have any direct contact with them after 1949. Some of these restrictions were removed in 1988.

Political stability and continuity have contributed to the development of an economic climate in Taiwan favorable to rapid industrial growth (Johnson, 1981). General elections were finally permitted in 1972, but the Kuomintang has remained in power with little effective opposition. Chiang Kai-Shek continued as President until his death, and one of his sons had held this office until recently. Cooperation between government and business is carried out through the Executive Yuan and a planning agency, the Ministry of Economic Affairs. The structure of the government is complex because the Nationalist Government and the National Assembly are still, theoretically, the government of the Republic of China (including the Mainland). The Provincial Government is the government of the Province of Taiwan, and there are various municipal and local governments that have considerable autonomy. The people elect representatives to the Provincial Government and local governments, including local community councils.

Taiwan was originally occupied by aboriginal tribes of unknown origin. There were explorations of the island from Mainland China as early as the third century B.C., but no significant migrations until Hakkas, fleeing persecution on the Mainland, established settlements before 1,000 A.D. During the Ming Dynasty (1368-1644) migration from Fukien province began. The modern Taiwanese dialect developed from Fukienese. In the West, word came from Portuguese sailors sailing to Japan about this "isla formosa" (beautiful island). Other nations became aware of the value and beauty of the island and attempted conquest; the Japanese in 1593, the Dutch in 1624, and the Spanish in the 1630s, but these occupations were short-lived. The Manchu invasion of Southern China brought the end of the Ming dynasty, and the last Ming general withdrew to Taiwan in 1658 with a large army and many followers. He captured the Dutch settlements, established the first formal Chinese government, and attempted to develop centers of Chinese culture on the island. Taiwan became part of the Chinese empire in 1684, when Manchu armies defeated the Ming forces. Taiwan was opened to foreign trade after the First Opium War in 1860, and British and American trade and missionary activity developed rapidly. Japanese interest in Taiwan was renewed, however; and in 1874, a Japanese army invaded Taiwan. The Chinese government negotiated a settlement that kept Taiwan as part of China until 1895, when the Japanese victory over China made Taiwan a Japanese possession. The fifty years of Japanese occupation saw the building of roads and railroads, schools, hospitals, and industries, and the updating of agricultural methods; but the resources of Taiwan were developed primarily for the benefit of the Japanese economy.

The return of Taiwan to China and the coming of Chiang Kai-Shek meant a return to Chinese culture as well as technological modernization. The Nationalists brought with them many of the great art treasures of the Mainland and a determination to make Taiwan the center of Chinese culture.

Confucianism has been the dominant ethical influence in daily life in Taiwan but has not become a formal religion, except in a few places. The tendency to blend traditional religions with popular or folk religion, which is found in other parts of China, is much in evidence in Taiwan. There are many temples in the cities and the rural villages. Much of the popular religion is identified with Buddhism, and there are many Buddhist temples. "Popular" Buddhism may contain beliefs and practices derived from animism, ancestor worship, Confucian customs, Taoist ideas, and folk religion. Folk religion may include local deities as well as some of the more common Chinese deities such as Kuan Yin (Goddess of Mercy) and Kuan Kung (originally a folk hero who distinguished himself as a soldier and martyr). Christian missionaries have been in Taiwan since the Dutch began efforts at colonization in the seventeenth century. Extensive missionary activity began after the end of the Second Opium War in 1860. The Christian presence remains numerically small although important through its influence on the Nationalist government and the development of schools, hospitals, and social service agencies. Some of our informants noted, however, that increasing numbers of Taiwanese identify themselves as having "no religion." Mainlanders who came from the classical Confucian tradition may also refuse to identify themselves with any formal religion.

SINGAPORE

Singapore is also an island, but a much smaller one (data in this section, unless otherwise noted, are from *Singapore Facts and Pictures, 1984*). The main island is about one-sixtieth the size of Taiwan (570 square kilometres compared to 35,571). There are fifty-seven small islets included in the Republic of Singapore that add a little to its territory. Singapore is not only smaller, but it is located much closer to the equator, about one degree north of the equator, which gives it a year-round tropical climate. The average daily temperature is 26.6 degrees Centigrade and the average humidity is 84.6 percent. Tropical downpours are frequent, and the average annual rainfall is more than ninety-three inches.

The visitor to Singapore is impressed with how modern, clean, and orderly the city is, with many wide tree-lined streets, beautiful parks, and carefully regulated traffic flow. Outside of the main business and shopping areas there are many "housing estates" with groupings of high rise apartment houses. There are some parts of the city that have private homes, but most of the people (80%) live in the publicly-funded housing projects in "flats" that they may purchase by borrowing from their account with the Central Provident Fund (retirement fund).

Singapore is essentially a city state, although some of the island is still under cultivation; and there are a few remaining semi-rural areas. More than half of the island has been developed for housing and industry, although there are some forested areas and marsh lands. It is the geographic location that has given Singapore its significance as a commercial and trade center. The island is located at the tip of the Malaysian Peninsula and is a natural center for shipping and trade between East Asia (China, Japan, Taiwan, and Korea) and South Asia (India and Ceylon). It is also a natural port for imports to and exports from the Malaysian Peninsula. Its immediate neighbors are West Malaysia (across a narrow causeway to the north), East Malaysia (Brunei, Sabah, Sarawak) and the Philippines across the South China Sea, and Indonesia (Sumatra across the Straits of Malacca and Borneo and Java across the South China Sea). With the development of world trade by sea and air, Singapore has become one of the great world centers of trade and commerce.

The potential importance of Singapore was first recognized by Sir Stamford Raffles of the British East India Company, who negotiated with the Sultan of Johor to establish a settlement. A trading station was established in 1819 under the jurisdiction of the East India Company. In 1826, it became part of the Straits Settlement. Until 1867, Singapore was under the British government of India; but in that year, control was transferred to the British Colonial Office. The importance of Singapore as a military base and trade center increased under British influence, especially after the opening of the Suez Canal in 1869. During the Second World War, however, Singapore fell to the Japanese and was occupied for three and a half years. After the war, Singapore became a British Crown Colony, but there was increasing agitation for self-government; and in 1948, a Legislative Council was created, which included some popularly elected representatives. A commission to draw up a constitution was created in 1953. When the proposed constitution was ratified by the British Parliament, Singapore became the State of Singapore in 1959. In 1961, a Federation of Malaysia was proposed, with Singapore as one of its members. The Federation came into being in 1963, but Singapore separated from the Federation in 1965 and became a fully independent and sovereign nation. On December 22, 1965, Singapore became a republic.

Since the first election in 1959, the Peoples' Action Party has controlled the Legislative Assembly and Lee Kwan Yew served as Prime Minister until 1990. Opposition parties are permitted, but no strong opposition has developed. Singapore has a parliamentary form of government, with a unicameral assembly elected every five years. Parliament may be dissolved, however; and then a general election must be held within three months.

The population of Singapore was about two and half million in 1983. Regulation of immigration and control of the birth rate have kept the population relatively constant. Most of the population is Chinese (76.6%). Malays constitute 14.7%, Indians (including Pakistanis, Bangladeshis, and Sri Lankans) make up 6.4%, and other ethnic groups 2.3%. There are four official languages: Malay, Mandarin, Tamil, and English. Malay is the national language, but English is the language of administration. Workers from other countries may be brought to Singapore if needed but may be returned to their country of origin at any time. Obtaining Singapore citizenship may be difficult for someone who was not born there of Singaporean parents. The Chinese came to Singapore from various parts of China and at different times. Most of the early immigrants were men. When immigration quotas were adopted in the 1930s, many women came. Immigration from China virtually came to an end after the Communist Revolution. The diversity of the earlier immigrants is reflected in the fact that there were reported to be twenty-six different Chinese dialects in Singapore when we were there in 1972, although three dialects–Hokkien, Cantonese, and Teochew–predominated.

The economy of Singapore has developed rapidly. There is virtually no unemployment, and wives are encouraged to work. In addition to the services needed in a large city, there is employment in the banking, commercial, and shipping activities of a large trade center; and a variety of industries has been developed. The housing and development policies have encouraged the establishment of industrial parks with high rise housing for workers. Many multinational corporations have branches in Singapore; and products from all over the world are to be found in the stores. It is our observation that the Japanese presence has increased markedly since 1972, and Japanese products of various kinds are much in evidence. Tourism is a major industry. Many large hotels have been built in recent years, and great efforts have been made to keep the city clean, orderly, and attractive. In addition to the large corporations and shiny new highrise shopping centers, the traditional family "shop house" is still found in many parts of Singapore. Some of the older streets are lined with small shops, and the families of the owners of these shops live in the same building, either behind the shops or on one of the floors above the shops. The floors above the shops may be divided into rooms or small apartments which are rented to individuals or families. The modernization of the city, however, has meant the demolition of some of the older neighborhoods and increasing concentration of small shops in highrise air-conditioned shopping centers. Many changes have taken place between the time of our first visit in 1972 and our most recent in 1991.

As in Taiwan, political stability and continuity and cooperation between government and business have been important in developing the industrial potential and the strategic commercial and trade possibilities of Singapore. Such a small nation cannot survive on its own resources and must compete successfully on the international trade routes and in the world markets. It must also maintain friendly ties with its larger neighbors. The various ministries in the government serve to plan and develop the limited space and resources of the island, to promote business and industry, to encourage trade and tourism, to provide for the defense of the island, and to provide necessary services for the protection and welfare of the people. Singapore is a member of the British Commonwealth of Nations and plays an active role in ASEAN (the Association of South East Asian Nations).

An educated work force is necessary for a country such as Singapore. The current educational system, adopted in 1979, is based on the British model. All children are expected to have a primary education. At the end of the third year they are channeled into bilingual or monolingual programs, based on their performance in the first three years. At the end of six years (eight for the monolingual program) students take a primary school leaving examination and are placed in secondary schools or vocational training schools. After four of five years (depending on the program) they take "0" level examinations which determine whether they will be admitted to "preuniversity" or "junior college" programs. Admission to the National University or the various technical institutes is highly competitive. Throughout the system the fate of the individual student is tied to his or her performance on the examinations, and much of the pressure at home and school is related to preparation for these examinations. There have been significant changes in the educational system since 1985. Increasing emphasis has been placed on mastery of mathematics and language, but the pattern of examinations continues to be important.

"Moral education" is now included for all students, and a special curriculum for "moral education" has been developed. It is also possible to enroll in Biblical, Buddhist, Hindu, Sikh, or Islamic studies, world religions, or Confucian ethics. As this diversity suggests, there is a wide variety of religious traditions represented in Singapore. There are many churches and temples; however, the schools established by missionaries have been supported by grants-in-aid since the colonial period, and the government controls the educational standards and syllabi (Wee, 1987). A few hospitals continue to be run by religious groups. It is interesting that the Ministry of Culture's *Singapore Facts and Pictures, 1984,* lists the various religious groups under the "Culture and Recreation" section but provides no statistical data concerning membership in the various groups. One of the interesting things about living in Singapore is becoming familiar with the holidays or festivals celebrated by the different religious and ethnic groups during the year.

Chapter Three

Aging in Traditional Chinese Society

THE FAMILY SYSTEM

Understanding of aging in Chinese society is closely tied to understanding of the Chinese family system. As Lin Yutang (1939) has said, ". . . the family system is the root of Chinese society, from which all Chinese characteristics derive" (p. 167).

The family system was organized for survival. Traditionally, it was both a social and economic unit. Family income and property were held in common under the direction of the male head of the family, whether the family property was a piece of land and the buildings on it or a family shop or business. The male head was responsible for the distribution of the family's income or products to the members as well as leading the family to improve its economic and social position. Each family was, ideally at least, a communal unit to which each contributed according to ability and from which each received according to need, with "need being interpreted in favor of males and elders" (Wee, 1987). The male head was responsible for organizing the family to perform its economic functions, although the running of the household usually was the responsibility of his wife (or his mother, if she was still alive).

The relationships between and among family members were defined primarily by their roles and functions within the family system. These roles and relationships were symbolized by kinship terms. Learning these terms and the appropriate roles and functions they symbolized was basic to appropriate behavior within the family system.

19

The structure of the family was hierarchical. At the top of the hierarchy, theoretically at least, were the oldest members of the family. The hierarchy among the elders was determined by the relationship of each elder to the patrilineal head of the family. Within the structure, the lines of authority-obedience were sharply drawn. The lineal head was the final authority, although he might chose to share his authority with his wife and also with other elders in the family. Within the community or village, authority for community affairs and public behavior was shared by elders from the various families under one primary authority figure. The model of family structure, roles, and relationships was basic to all levels of common life–local, regional, and national. In some form, this pattern of social organization of human relationships has been part of Chinese life for many centuries.

The philosophical and ethical foundations of the Chinese pattern of social relationships are attributed primarily to the teachings of Confucius and his followers. Confucius endeavored to establish ethical principles that would promote peace and harmony in social relationships. He emphasized appropriate behavior or ''propriety'' (*li*) in the five Cardinal Relationships–relations between ruler and subject, husband and wife, parent and child, elder sibling and younger sibling, and friends. The ideal of fully human person (*ren* or *jen*) knows his place in all human situations and shows kindness, benevolence, or ''human-heartedness'' to other persons in ways that are appropriate to each situation (Reid, 1984, pp. 63-70).

THE MEANING OF THE FAMILY IN CHINESE CULTURE

The family is an economic and social unit, but the meaning of ''family'' in a Chinese sense is difficult to describe in American or Western terms. ''Family'' is a kind of mythical entity that has meaning far beyond economic and biological ties. It is the primary context of the meaning of life. It has to do with a lineage that stretches far back into the past and will continue into the future. The current family and its members find their place within that lineage and contribute what they can to the ongoing welfare and reputation (''face'') of the family. The family is the basic entity of life, and the individual is defined by his or her place in the family and his or her contribution to the family's maintenance and advancement. The individual does not exist as a person in his or her own right in the Western sense.

Lin Yutang (1939), in his interpretation of traditional Chinese society, *My Country and My People*, writes:

> . . . the Chinese family system . . . was so well defined and organized as to make it impossible for a man to forget where his lineage belonged. This form of social immortality, which the Chinese prize above all earthly possessions, has something of the character of a religion, which is enhanced by the ritual of ancestor worship, and the consciousness of it has penetrated deep into the Chinese soul. (p. 35)

Margery Wolf (1968) talks about the meaning of family when she describes the home of the Chinese family with whom she lived in Taiwan from 1959-1961. She is describing the memorial tablets of departed family members that stood on the altar table in the entrance hall:

> Individually, the tablets have little significance. They are simply a focal point for burning offerings in honor of the parent who was respected if not loved. Collectively, however, they are the symbol of something larger. They are the proof of an unbroken chain of men beginning in a distant past of splendid achievements, a past in which the insignificant farmer burning incense was represented by his own blood relatives even though not himself present. Through him and because of him the chain will pass to his son and his son's sons into an equally splendid world of the future in which he will again be represented though not present. For many Taiwanese, both the humble who accept their religion without question and the sophisticated who scoff at its mysticism, it is this concept of being one link in an awesomely long chain, unimportant in themselves yet essential to the continuation of the chain, that gives meaning to what might be an unkind world of hard work and hunger. (pp. 25, 26)

F.L.K. Hsu (1963), an American anthropologist of Chinese ancestry, writes in a more pragmatic manner about the meaning of family. He is talking about the extended family writ large as the "clan"–the families who trace their origin to a common location and a common ancestor and share an ancestral hall, graveyard, genealogy, and family legends:

> . . . as soon as a member of a clan becomes well-to-do, and especially if he achieves some prominence through the examination system, he tends to spare no effort in rebuilding his clan ancestral hall, widening the genealogical records, and generally improving or strengthening the organization and affairs of his clan. All this he does by following the ideal model set forth by his ancestors, according to the classics. In so doing he is not necessarily moved by altruism. On the one hand he will derive great pride from being a member of a prosperous clan with its many external signs of affluence. On the other hand, he is discharging his duties toward his forebears according to his ability, exactly as he expects his descendants to discharge theirs in the years to come. The better example he sets himself to be, the greater is the likelihood that his descendants will follow in his footsteps. For in viewing life, he is thinking of the future not less than the past, but his concept of both is channelled into the narrow familial and clan path. (pp. 117, 118)

AGING IN THE CHINESE FAMILY

Within the context of the family, in its ideal form at least, the position of the aging members was clearly defined and relatively secure. The ongoing life of the family was governed by the mutual obligations that family members had to each other. The older members were expected to care for the younger ones until they could care for themselves. In turn, the younger members were expected to care for the older ones when they were in need of care, and all remained dependent upon the family to provide for their needs. "Filial piety" and "respect for elders" were learned in childhood.

The role, status, and authority of the elders were defined by the traditional family system, although it was sometimes recognized that there might be conditions under which elders might not be able to exercise their authority effectively. The deceased members of the family were idealized and held up as examples or models, and the elders who were still alive shared in this idealization process.

Pearl Buck (1960), who spent the early years of her life with Chinese children in her parents' missionary compound, described what it meant to her to grow up learning a Chinese sense of her place in the family:

> A child learned in the home how to conduct himself toward the different generations of grandparents and parents, elder and younger uncles and aunts, elder and younger cousins and brothers and sisters and servants; and in school, he learned how to conduct himself toward teachers and friends, and officials and neighbors and acquaintances. Being so taught, the youth was never ill at ease, never uncertain of how to behave or how to speak to anyone. The essential rules were simple and clarified by the usage of centuries, and so the growing personality was poised and calm. (p. 15)
>
> . . . I am glad that my first years were in an ordered world, for though it passed, still the memory holds of what it means to a child to live in such a world, where adults were calm and confident and where children knew the boundaries beyond which they could not go and within which they lived secure. (p. 17)

In the context of an extended family "long life" was considered to be a blessing for anyone. An older male member of the family might have brothers and their wives and children sharing the same house along with his own married sons and their wives and children and his unmarried daughters. He might even have an elderly parent still living, if he was not the surviving elder himself. His wife and the brothers' wives had each other for company and their children and grandchildren to show them affection and respect, with the younger wives and the servants to perform the more mundane household chores. "Long life" was idealized, of course; and poverty, poor health, physical limitations, and family conflict could keep longevity from being far from ideal. On the family farm or in the family enterprise, however, if the elders were healthy and able, there were jobs that they could do and their opinions were important. Much of the actual oversight of small children was their responsibility, since the childrens' parents were usually busy with the work of the fields, the shop, or the house. In the traditional family, the elders had a place of honor and respect. They were the authoritative representatives of the family traditions and ideals, and they had important functions to perform as long as they were able to do so. In a patrilineal and patrilocal culture, the ideals of "long life" were oriented toward men; and life could be difficult for an elderly woman, particularly if she had no sons or no male grandchildren. In the extended family, however, there was usually work for the widow to do, and she could have a place of some honor in her later years.

ELDERS WITHOUT FAMILIES

The family was the primary means of support for the elderly. Although an older person without family might share the honor and respect for all older persons in the community, having some kind of family ties was important for security in the later years of life. If for some reason older persons did not have family of their own but belonged to a strong clan, the clan organization might take responsibility for their support (Jernigan, 1976). For elders who lived in a city and did not have a family of their own or belong to a clan, there were two kinds of substitutes for the clan organization: (1) the regional or district organizations of persons who shared a common place of origin and (2) the surname organizations of persons who shared a common surname regardless of their place of origin. These organizations varied in the amount of support that they provided for an individual member, but they did perform some of the functions of an extended family (Ikels, 1983, pp. 26, 27). Women who did not marry sometimes joined peer organizations or sisterhoods, often with other women who participated in the same kind of work. Membership was lifelong and members provided various kinds of support for each other, especially if they shared a common residence. There were also some forms of male "brotherhoods" in which men, who for some reason had no family or had left their families, joined together. These various kinds of family substitutes operated on the principle of "reciprocity" or mutual obligation of members to provide support for each other (Wong, 1982).

The experience of being without family was one to be avoided if possible, and individuals in such a situation might seek to adopt a child in order to have someone to care for them in old age. Instead of adoption, a *kai* relationship, vaguely similar to our "godparent" relationship, might be developed. An older person would provide care and attention to a younger person who had special needs. The younger person might continue to live with his or her own family but receive gifts and special attention from the *kai* "parent" on birthdays and other significant occasions. If the younger person had no parents, care received from the older person would mean an obligation to reciprocate when the elder could no longer care for himself or herself (Ikels, 1983, p. 21). Regarding the *kai* relationship, Wee comments concerning the common pattern (1987):

> . . . the *kai* "parent" is a childless/single friend of natural parents who are overburdened with expenses of child-rearing. The *kai* parent helps out with school/living expenses, earning reciprocal care in old age.

THE ELDERLY IN THE CITY

China before the Communist revolution was predominantly rural, and the most common context for aging was the farm or village family. Extended families did live in cities, of course, and the patterns of family life were similar to those found in rural areas but were tied to the family shop or business rather than the family farm. Young people who came to the city to find work, however, sent money home to their families regularly, visited often, and were expected to return to their village when they were no longer working in the city. They might belong to a clan, a district, or a surname association, as described above; but their primary ties were with their families of origin and their home villages. Those who chose to remain in the cities sought to establish their own extended families and to bring siblings and parents to live with them if possible.

For city dwellers without families, the voluntary associations might be important, or they might join some kind of peer organization with fellow workers. Individuals who were without family but had established strong ties with a city family, shop, or business might continue such a relationship until death. They would perform less work as the years went by but would continue to do some kind of work as long as they were physically able. To be an anonymous elder in the city without strong connections with family, peers, or employer, however, could be a very unpleasant fate (Ikels, 1983, pp. 25-28).

THE "GOOD LIFE"

We have seen some of the potentialities for a long life as a good life in the family surrounded by children and grandchildren and enjoying a place of honor and respect in family and community. The Confucian emphasis on propriety and the virtues of reciprocity and filial piety were important for the continuing support and respect of the elders.

Confucius' ideal of the mature adult, as expressed in the *Analects* (1938), reflected the importance of the elder being able to learn propriety as a youth and to develop a harmonious inner life that could be expressed in appropriate conduct as the years went by:

> At fifteen, I set my heart upon learning. At thirty, I had planted my feet firmly upon the ground. At forty, I no longer suffered from perplexities. At fifty, I knew what were the biddings of Heaven. At sixty, I heard them with docile ear. At seventy, I could follow the dictates of my own heart; for what I desired no longer overstepped the boundaries of right. (2:4)

Chapter Four

Two Rapidly Changing Chinese Societies

INTRODUCTION

From our previous studies and experience in Singapore and our continuing studies of Chinese culture, we were somewhat familiar with the place of elders in the family system. We were also aware that both Taiwan and Singapore had undergone rapid and radical changes of many kinds. We were interested in learning what we could about the impact of these changes on the Chinese family, particularly on the experience of aging in the context of the family.

One of the difficulties we soon encountered was what is meant by "old age" and "the elderly." In Taiwan, we learned that, although retirement age is sixty-five for most persons employed in government, education, business, or industry, a person is not considered "elderly" until age seventy. The "Law of the Aged Peoples' Welfare," that was promulgated in 1980, refers to persons seventy or older. In Singapore, on the other hand, the retirement age was fifty-five, although the more common retirement age is now sixty (Wee, 1987). Some studies of aging in Singapore are concerned with persons age fifty-five and older. Others focus on persons age sixty and above.

Neither Taiwan nor Singapore has an aging population of the same magnitude as the United States. In the United States, a little over 12% of the population is sixty-five or older (19-20% in some of the suburban areas around Boston where we live). In Taiwan, about 4.5% of the population was sixty-five or older. In Singapore, a little under 5% were in this age group in 1985. The proportion of

27

those sixty-five and above in Taiwan was somewhat skewed by the number of elderly veterans who came over from the Mainland with Chiang Kai-Shek's army in 1949 and could not return to the Mainland. In both countries, the life expectancy is approaching that of the United States, and more and more people are living into their seventies, eighties, and nineties. The predictions are that the proportion of older persons in the populations will increase significantly between now and the year 2000. This projected change in the populations is of concern to students of aging everywhere.

SOME IMPORTANT CHANGES: INDUSTRIALIZATION, URBANIZATION, AND FAMILY MOBILITY

As we have seen, traditional views of the Chinese family reflected a relatively stable society in which most families lived in small villages and worked on family farms. Cities existed, of course; but even here, the family shop or small business was common. The development of modern industries and large scale business enterprises has created the possibilities of increased incomes and higher standards of living in Taiwan and Singapore but also the need for workers to live in urban areas.

In Taiwan the pace of change has been rapid. In 1952, the net value of domestic products was 364 million U.S. dollars, of which 36% was from agriculture, and 18% was from industry. In 1983, the value of domestic products had risen to almost 50 billion dollars, of which less than 8% was from agriculture, and 50% was from industry. Similarly, the nature of the work force had changed radically in thirty years. In 1952, 61% of the work force was employed in agriculture and 9% in industry; while in 1983 less than 19% was in agriculture and 41% in industry (Chao, 1984, p. 6). Thirty years ago most people lived in rural areas; but by 1980, according to our informants, more than 70% of the people lived in cities with populations of 20,000 or more.

The reality of such statistics is that in a thirty year period Taiwan changed from a predominantly rural agricultural society to one that is predominantly urban and industrial. This change has meant that many people either have left the farm or have taken another job in addition to farm work. The image of an entire extended family working together on a farm and living together under one roof is rapidly disappearing. Agriculture and the farm are still important; but, for people to participate in Taiwan's rising standard of living, more than farm income may be needed. Often the children of farmers and, sometimes, the farmers themselves have gone to where the jobs are. On a farm we visited on the outskirts of Taipei, three brothers work together part-time in the rice fields; but two of them live in the city, and all three hold jobs in industry.

Life in the city for most families means living in an apartment or "flat" rather than in their own house. It often means that both parents are away from the apartment ten or twelve hours a day, including commuting time. The children are in school most of the day and busy with studies when they come home. If they are approaching college age, they may be involved in additional studies to prepare for entrance examinations. If they are finishing college, they may be preparing for examinations to study in the United States or Canada. Grandparents may have responsibility for the care of small children and older children when they are home from school, but adolescents may spend little time at home. When the children leave home for college or jobs or marriage, there may be little for the grandparents to do.

There are many variations on this situation, both in Taiwan and Singapore. In Singapore, the process of urbanization and industrialization has been going on longer, and there has not been much of a rural population in recent times. The "kampongs" (rural or semi-rural close-knit communities) that once existed have almost all been demolished to make way for industry or modern housing developments. The "kampong" families have had to move to high rise "flats" built by the government, which they rent or purchase. Some of the older parts of the city that contained "shophouses" and small apartments have also been demolished to make way for more modern housing and shopping centers. Singapore is a city that is continually changing and becoming more modern, but it has had a relatively stable urbanized population for the last thirty years. Most of the Chinese immigrants to Singapore came before 1949, and there has been increasing control over immigration since that time.

The extended family has continued to be important in Singapore, even though not usually living under one roof. In recent years, the government has tried to encourage adult members of an extended family to live in nearby or adjacent flats by giving them priority in housing; and in 1987, the first "granny suite" flats were developed, providing a connected large and small flat, each with its own front door (Wee, 1987). Even without such encouragement by the government, however, there is evidence that family members tend to live in reasonably close proximity to each other, at least in the same postal zone (Wong and Kuo, 1979, quoted in Wee, 1983). Travel to the flats of family members is relatively easy, and telephone communication is increasing. Parents are available to care for the children of their married offspring and may continue to have much of the responsibility for rearing their grandchildren. Increasingly, retired adults may also have the responsibility of caring for their own aging parents.

In the larger cities of Taiwan, travel to reach the apartments of family members is more difficult and there are fewer telephones. The most common pattern, however, is for elders who do not continue to live on the family farm to live with one of their adult children in the city, sometimes on a rotating basis, and to have child care responsibilities as long as these are needed. Even if retired parents do not live with their adult children, frequent contact may continue and child care arrangements may be made. The children are expected to care for their elderly parents, and the employment situation may require the elders to provide child care whenever possible.

The decrease in family-oriented functions of retired family members under the working and living conditions of urban families, especially as the grandchildren grow older, leaves many elders with little that is important to do. Women may be able to continue to be busy with sewing, cooking, and other domestic skills; but men may have difficulty finding much to do around an apartment, depending on their interests and hobbies, of course. Activities with other elders who share common interests (and a common dialect in Singapore) may become increasingly important, and we shall note later how the governments of both Taiwan and Singapore are trying to encourage the development of peer groups of various kinds. Elders who live on the farm may continue to have important functions to perform, depending on their physical ability, but family division is common and various arrangements are made to support elders who can no longer support themselves (Hsieh, 1984).

Technological changes in family living have also had an impact on the experience of the elderly members. The telephone has made possible communication between family members who no longer live together but also may reduce the need or motivation for face-to-face contact. The development of radio and television communication and the increasing availability of radios, TVs, and video cassette recorders makes it possible for elders to find forms of entertainment at home that did not exist earlier and may reduce the need for socialization. In Singapore, the variations in the availability of radio and TV programs and video cassettes in the many Chinese dialects limit the use of such resources by the elderly members of some dialect groups.

Respect for elders continues to be an important emphasis in the Chinese societies of Taiwan and Singapore, but the changes in the roles and functions of older persons are creating new problems. Urban living can mean significant changes in the family pattern of authority. The elder members may continue to have primary authority on the family farm or in the family shop; but in an apartment, the elders may not have much actual authority. They are living in someone else's space; the family income may come primarily from other family members; and the children are out of sight and beyond their control much of the time. If the older members arise early and go to bed early, there may be little opportunity for communication with the younger members who are working long hours or involved with school and homework.

In Singapore, communication between the generations may be a real problem because of language barriers. The older members of the family often speak the dialect of the region of China from which they came. The younger members, particularly the grand-children, may have little understanding (or appreciation) of such a dialect. The only form of Chinese that they learn at school is Mandarin. They also learn English, but the older generation may know little Mandarin or English. The language problem usually does not exist in Taiwan. Families speak either Mandarin or Taiwanese, or sometimes both; but there is an increasing generation gap because of Western influences on the younger generation and the rapid changes of urban living.

Chapter Five

Aging in Rapidly Changing Chinese Societies: A Summary and Interpretation of Our Study

INTRODUCTION

One of our interviewees in Taiwan gave us a graphic picture of a lifestyle that honors the traditional Chinese understanding of filial relationships to mother/grandmother but which, in actuality, offers little time for relationships between the mother/grandmother and her children and grandchildren, even though they live in the same apartment. Another interviewee, a man from a farm family which was now divided between one brother who continued to live on the farm and the other brothers who lived and worked in the city, expressed little hope that he would have any influence over his grandchildrens' vocational future. He said, "They will do what they want to do."

These responses are not necessarily typical, but they do highlight some of the issues involved in older persons' experiences of a rapidly changing culture. We want to summarize some of the things that we learned in Taiwan and Singapore and that seem important to share. We recognize the difficulties of generalizing on the basis of our limited sample, but we have supplemented our interviews with data and impressions from other sources. In this chapter, we

33

will summarize what we have learned; and in the next chapter, we will focus on the experiences of individuals as shared with us in our interviews in Taiwan. The information and impressions in this chapter are based on:

1. our previous experience living and working in Singapore
2. our background readings
3. our interviews with elders and with resource persons in Taiwan
4. reports of interviews with elders in a farm village (Hsieh, 1984) and a fishing village (Chuang, 1984) in Taiwan
5. a report of interviews with elders in the "Chinatown" section of Singapore (Wong, 1982)
6. the *Report on the National Survey of Senior Citizens*, Singapore Ministry of Social Affairs, 1983 and the *Report of the Committee on the Problems of the Aged*, Ministry of Health, 1984
7. interviews with resource persons in Singapore
8. personal correspondence with one of our resource persons in Singapore (Wee, 1987).

This summary is organized in terms of the interactions of personality and culture around the four aspects of personhood that were outlined in Chapter One. Such a summary obviously does not do justice to the differences in the experiences of individual persons, and we will focus on some of these differences in the next chapter.

PHYSICAL SURVIVAL

Our previous studies of ethnicity and aging have suggested that the following aspects of the experience of the elderly are important for physical survival–income, diet, housing, transportation, medical care, sleep, exercise, and safety. We have organized our data and reflections under each of these headings.

Income

One of the assumptions of Chinese society in both Taiwan and Singapore is that income is family income, not individual income, and elders in the family are entitled to share in family income. Filial piety and the mutual obligations of family members to care for each other mean that children are to provide for their parents financially if parents cannot provide for themselves. In Taiwan, this obligation is recognized legally in Book IV of the Civil Code. The Committee on the Problems of the Aged in Singapore recommended the adoption of a similar legal recognition of the financial obligations of family life (1984, p. 43).

The Singapore Committee recognized that filial piety cannot be legislated. The appropriate attitudes and values are necessary; and if these are not present, a legal requirement may have little force. The Committee emphasized the importance of individuals learning the necessary attitudes and values in the context of the family, the school, and the community. The Committee's emphasis on attitudes and values highlights the problem of changing attitudes and values and changing family lifestyles under the conditions of the rapid cultural change that has been occurring in Taiwan and Singapore. What is happening to the family affects every aspect of the experience of the older members. More will be said about this in later sections. At this point, we are concerned about what influences the ability of the elders to cope with their survival needs.

The rapidly rising standard of living in Taiwan and Singapore, in which most families participate, has meant that most older family members have reasonable financial resources to meet their needs. This was true of the persons we interviewed in Taiwan and, for the most part, of the persons (more than 90%) included in the National Survey in Singapore. We recognize, however, the existence of indigent elders living alone without families and families, that may, for various reasons, have limited means to support elderly members.

The Central Provident Fund (CPF) was established in Singapore in 1955 in order that workers might have their own income to supplement family support and/or to contribute to family resources when they retire. Only 7% of the persons included in the Survey had the CPF as a source of reserve funds, but the CPF will be of value to future generations of elders. For the first ten years, CPF contributions were very small. It was not until the mid 1970s that both wages and CPF contribution rates rose sharply. Elders surveyed in 1983 were the generation born too early to benefit from the CPF. It was not until the late 1980s that retired workers began to receive substantial amounts of money (Wee, 1987).

Taiwan has established a social insurance program, which included about four million workers in 1984 and was being expanded in 1985. The retired teachers and government workers among our interviewees had benefited from this program, which included options for a lump sum payment on retirement or pension payments throughout their lifetime. They had all opted to receive a lump sum payment. The two veterans had military pensions, and one woman had a pension from the industry in which her husband had worked.

We need to recognize that the sense of security of the individual in Taiwan is tied to their sense of security about the future of their island republic. The close proximity of the Mainland, the size of the population of the Peoples' Republic of China and its military power make the political and economic future of Taiwan uncertain. This uncertainty is at least part of the reason that people like our interviewees opted for a lump sum payment rather than a monthly pension.

Although most of the respondents to the National Survey in Singapore did not report inadequate income to meet their needs, the Committee on the Problems of the Aged in Singapore, looking to the future, recommended continued part-time or full-time employment for older workers as long as possible. Such employment would, of course, add to the older workers' financial resources, but the Committee also saw it as contributing to the workers' general well-being. Changing the retirement age (at which persons can make withdrawals from the Central Provident Fund) from fifty-five to sixty-five was also recommended. Such a recommendation makes assumptions about the importance of work for the mental and physical well-being of older persons as well as their financial status. It may also involve assumptions about the value of the continuing contributions of older persons to their places of employment, although the Committee's report talks of older persons returning to work at jobs which pay less than the ones they had had before retirement. Regardless of the value of these recommendations to the workers or the work place, however, the recommendations assume an economy that is continually expanding and has room both for older workers and the younger ones coming into the work force. The economic recession that Singapore was experiencing in the mid 1980s raised questions about such an assumption. The rate of economic growth of Taiwan was also slowing down in 1985, but Taiwan authorities might be in a better position to consider the kind of recommendation the Singapore Committee was making. It is clear, however, that such a recommendation would be of much greater benefit to men than women because of the disparities between the numbers of older men and women in the work force. As Barbara Myerhoff (1978) and Margery Wolf (1972) have pointed out, there may be less need for older women to be employed outside the home because of the kinds of activities that they are accustomed to undertaking at home. As the need for such activities decreases and lifestyles change in the cities, however, employment for women may become an increasing concern.

Both pension payments and income from continued employment are ways of helping older persons to have some independent income. In the studies of rural villages in Taiwan to which we had access, it was observed that some independent income seemed to be important to the psychological and social well-being of retired persons (Chang, 1984 and Hsieh, 1984).

Assuming that under "normal" circumstances in Taiwan and Singapore family support, or a combination of family support and individual resources, can be adequate to meet the financial needs of older persons, there are some special situations that these resources cannot meet. The most obvious situation is catastrophic or chronic illness. An accident or a major illness can be costly, and the cost may exhaust both individual and family resources. A chronic illness, such as Alzheimer's disease, may also be very costly, and the cost may continue for years. Only in rare circumstances would individual and family resources be adequate to meet the continuing cost. A terminal illness, such as some forms of cancer, may also be very expensive and may exhaust financial resources before death finally occurs. With more family members living longer, the likelihood of an expensive injury or illness becomes greater; and it is unrealistic to assume that family resources can bear all the burden. There are health care issues as well as financial support issues involved in such situations, but money is the "bottom line." Many countries are facing the question of where the money is to come from to meet the increasing costs of chronic or catastrophic illness in their older citizens.

Another situation that may render family financial resources inadequate is the long-lived "survivor." With persons living into their eighties and nineties, and even to be one hundred plus, it is possible for a family member to outlive all the other family members and to exhaust a family's financial resources. This may be an unusual situation in Taiwan and Singapore; but it is occurring with greater frequency in other countries and will occur more often in these two countries.

Nutrition

Our interviews in Taiwan and the National Survey in Singapore did not ask specifically about the diet of older persons. The general well-being of older persons in both countries, we assume, means that they have enough to eat. Nutrition may be a problem in other ethnic groups because of the inadequate diet of some persons living alone, but the Chinese cultural patterns greatly reduce the number of persons living alone. However, the Prime Minister's "1982 New Year Address to the People of Singapore" noted almost 14,000 households with couples or widows/widowers over the age of fifty living alone, and the Committee on the Problems of the Aged recognized that there were individuals and couples living alone who would benefit from some kind of meal delivery program.

Nutrition is partly a cultural concern, depending upon the adequacy of the diet of a particular ethnic group and the eating patterns of families. A wide variety of fresh fruits and vegetables and other kinds of foodstuff was available in both Taiwan and Singapore, but we have no data by which to evaluate the nutritional value of the diets of older persons. It was interesting to note that in the proposed health maintenance program, the Committee on the Problems of the Aged in Singapore did not include any suggestions for nutrition counseling. Such counseling may not be needed in Taiwan and Singapore, but there is world-wide concern about the relations of nutrition to the aging process; and we feel that no nation can afford to ignore the research that is being conducted and the implications that it may have for the diet of older persons.

Housing

Housing, like food, did not seem to be a problem for our interviewees in Taiwan, nor for most of the persons included in the National Survey in Singapore. It is clear that most elderly Chinese prefer to live with family members. Our informants in Taiwan told us, however, of increasing numbers of older persons who did not desire to live with their families. Housing for such persons on a "self-pay" basis was being developed in the cities. Few Chinese elders (2% according to the Singapore Survey data) want to live in an institution. In both countries, however, there was both public and private housing for the destitute poor.

In Singapore, efforts were being made to permit extended families to live in "flats" in close proximity, which is a change in earlier policies that mixed families and ethnic groups in public housing developments. It is also an attempt to reverse the trend toward nuclear family patterns and is tied to an effort to re-emphasize the Confucian value of "filial piety." As noted earlier, the first "granny suite flats" became available in 1987 (Wee, 1987). The recommendation of the Committee on the Problems of the Aged that retired persons be permitted to exchange their "flats" for smaller ones, if they desire, and use the difference in price to increase their Central Provident Fund annuity may or may not fit with this extended family policy. Even before the government policy was changed, the efforts of members of extended families were to obtain flats reasonably close to each other (Wee, 1983).

The adjustment to living in high rise flats is difficult for people who have been used to living in a community with their neighbors and close to the soil. Such an adjustment may be particularly difficult for older persons who may be left alone in the flat for long periods of time. During our visits to Singapore, we often heard concerns about the sterility and loneliness of living in a flat.

Transportation

The ability of Chinese elders to depend upon family members or public transportation if they had no means of transportation of their own was clear in our Taiwan interviews. In Taiwan, the *Law of the Aged People's Welfare* (1983) provided for half-fare on all forms of public transportation for persons seventy and above; and in the city of Taipei, they were entitled to free bus transportation. In Singapore, persons age sixty and above are entitled to receive a bus card that permits them to ride the buses at a reduced fare during off-peak hours (Wee, 1987). From our experience, we know of the availability of reliable and inexpensive bus transportation in Taipei, Taichung, and Singapore and the availability of relatively inexpensive (by American standards) taxis. In 1985, a subway system was in the process of construction in Singapore. From our studies of ethnicity and aging in other cities, however, we are aware that riding public transportation may be difficult for people who have physical limitations or who, for some reason, have difficulty coping with crowded streets and crowded buses or subway cars. In the Singapore Survey sample, increasing numbers of elders age seventy and above expressed fears of riding the public buses (age 70-74, 25%; age 75 and above, 46%). With an increasingly older population, both Taiwan and Singapore, like many other countries, may have to give more attention to the transportation needs of older persons. The important variable in Chinese societies is the ability of older persons to rely on family transportation when they can no longer make use of public transportation. The increasing isolation of elders from other family members during the day may mean that family transportation is not available for emergencies or for the kinds of regular trips that frail elders need to take in the daytime. The development of transportation services similar to those available in American cities for the elderly and the handicapped may become a necessity.

Medical Care

Our interviewees in Taiwan emphasized the importance of health. They could do what they were doing because they enjoyed reasonably good health. Two of the women with whom we talked, however, were responsible for the care of partially paralyzed husbands. Such a responsibility had obvious effects on their lifestyle. One woman had had a long and difficult struggle to raise her family and educate her children, but at the time of our interview was enjoying life with her son's family in spite of her husband's long-standing illness. The other woman had adequate resources from her husband's retirement income and was continuing to be active in her church. Family resources for medical care were adequate in both of these instances; but, with an increasingly older population, family resources may not be adequate for the kinds of catastrophic or chronic illness we noted earlier (p. 45).

Insurance programs that included medical benefits were being developed in Taiwan; and in Singapore, a portion of the total contributions to the Central Provident Fund were being set aside for medical care. Only a small proportion of the elders surveyed in Singapore in 1983 (less than 10%) had any kind of health insurance, however. For the most part older persons in Taiwan and Singapore must rely on their own and family resources to meet the costs of medical care. Free annual checkups are available to the elders in Taiwan once they reach the age of seventy, and there are clinics with subsidized health care available in the cities. Senior Citizens Health Care Centres are being developed in Singapore. Ten such centres are planned to be in operation by 1990 (Wee, 1987). Institutions for the sick elderly are also available; but, as we have seen, elderly Chinese do not like to be in institutions. The Singapore Committee on the Problems of the Aged recommended a comprehensive health maintenance program and the development of resources which would help the sick elderly to remain in their own homes as long as possible. We heard much concern about health among the elders we interviewed in Taiwan, and we saw efforts they were making, such as the exercise programs, to participate in their own health maintenance; however, the number of elders in Singapore who reported participating in exercise programs in their leisure time (less than 9%) was not encouraging. The recommendations of the Singapore Committee on health maintenance and the prevention of illness seemed to us to be commendable and compatible with the goals of family welfare and community development that were stated by the Commissioner of the Provincial Department of Social Affairs in Taiwan (Chao, 1983). We have continuing concern, however, about the future costs of chronic and catastrophic illness in the elderly population in both countries.

We have little information about environmental and lifestyle concerns that affect the health of elderly persons. We are aware, however, of the importance of clean air and water for all persons, particularly for the elderly. We know that air pollution can contribute to the health problems of elders who have developed any kind of respiratory difficulty. The pollution of the air in and around the cities in Taiwan is a concern for all age groups. In Singapore, the prevailing winds help to blow away many of the air pollutants, but there is a lot of automobile traffic, as well as industrial smoke. The quality of the air may be a concern. Smoking tobacco is a continuing health problem in both countries.

Sleep and Exercise

Our interviewees did not talk of sleep as a problem, and the Singapore Survey did not ask about sleep patterns. The most common pattern for our interviewees, as we noted, was to awake and arise early in the morning. Those early morning hours before anyone else is awake may be a problem, however, particularly for an older person who is somewhat depressed. Some of our sample talked of getting up early and going for a walk. Others talked about early morning exercise programs. We observed such programs in both Taiwan and Singapore. The early morning hours make sense when the climate is hot, as it is all year round in Singapore and during the summer in Taiwan. The Committee on the Problems of the Aged in Singapore recommended the establishment of exercise programs, along with other kinds of recreational activities, in all communities. They did not say at what time of day such programs should be offered. If the data from the Survey are to be believed, it may take major educational and promotional efforts for the majority of the elderly to participate in regular exercise programs.

One of the problems noted in our interviews was the difference in the sleep patterns of different generations living together as a family. The elders tend to go to bed earlier and to arise earlier than other family members. This pattern may limit the opportunities for interactions between the generations during the work week when the younger members of the family spend long hours during the day at work or at school.

Safety

Safety at home and on the streets is of concern to American elderly, particularly those living in cities (Harris et al., 1975). We do not have any data about the views of elders concerning safety in Taiwan and Singapore. The presence of other family members may make safety less of an issue, but we do know that elders are often alone in flats and on the streets during the day. The dangers of crime and vandalism in the flats and of accidents or muggings on the streets may need to be considered if urban living in Taiwan and Singapore becomes more like urban living in the United States. Statistics concerning road accidents in Singapore show that the elderly population is one of the vulnerable groups (Wee, 1987). The issue of safety is also an issue concerning the nature of the housing in which older persons live. Prevention of accidents in the home requires careful planning for housing for elders. Assistance once an accident occurs in the home may require some kind of regular daily contact with elders who spend much time alone.

SOCIALIZATION

In most cultures, support groups are necessary for survival; and in Chinese culture, the primary support group for many centuries has been the extended family. But the family also meets other kinds of needs—needs for physical contact, affection, recognition, belonging, and validation, as well as support. In the kind of situation that some of the immigrants to Singapore faced when they left families behind, a peer group became a substitute for a family; and there have been traditional ways to adopt a family if blood relatives were not available (Ikels, 1983, pp. 20, 21).

It is increasingly difficult for the family to be the primary source of social and emotional satisfactions under the conditions of rapid urbanization and industrialization in Taiwan and Singapore. When the family lived on its own land and the land was passed down from generation to generation, the ties of the family members to each other and to their land could be primary. In a somewhat similar way, ties to a family shop or business provided a common focus for the generations. When a family lives in a flat in the city, however, the younger members tend to go their various ways–to work, to school, to activities–during the day. There is little that is shared in common, and older members are left to their own devices. For an older woman, home care and child care may take up most of her time, when her grandchildren are small. Care for a sick or disabled spouse or an elderly parent may also occupy much of the daily routine. But, as the years go by, the older members of the family may have decreasing contact with children and grandchildren, or with their own elderly parent(s), and may have fewer and fewer tasks that are important to do. An apartment or flat may become a very small and isolated world. The danger, that we have seen among elders in American cities, particularly elders from family-oriented ethnic groups, is that the older person who spends great amounts of time alone in a flat may have so little social stimulation that various kinds of mental and physical deterioration may accelerate.

In this situation, the possibility of peer relationships becomes increasingly important, and activities with peers outside the home may be a significant way to occupy daytime hours. In Taiwan, the development of the "Long Life Clubs" and the activity centers or "Evergreen Academies" under government sponsorship recognized and encouraged peer activities and relationships. In Singapore, the community centers, various kinds of organizations which include older persons, and the informal "void deck" groups (meeting in the open space or "void deck" on the ground floor of some of the high rise apartment houses) also permitted and encouraged peer relation-ships. Churches and temples were also natural places for elders to gather with other persons in their age group who share some of their values and interests. Our interviewees in Taiwan included persons involved in activity centers, church organizations, and other volunteer activities, as well as some whose life was almost entirely focused in a family or a family business.

The Singapore Survey did not ask about participation in group activities, although we had information about a wide variety of volunteer activities available for elders. The most popular leisure time activities were not group activities, however. They were watch-ing television or video, listening to the radio, and going for walks. The next three most popular activities were more social–sitting in parks/coffee shops, going to places of worship, and visiting with friends. The implications of this data for the social and emotional needs of the elderly need further exploration. The recommendations of the Singapore Committee on the Problems of the Aged for con-tinuing employment for older workers, who are mostly male, may, indirectly at least, say something about the importance of work relationships in meeting the needs of men for peer relationships. The retired man can easily be an isolated man in the city.

The traditional patterns of social relationships for Chinese elderly emphasized family and village ties. In Chapter Three, we discussed some of the ways in which the elderly in the cities met their social needs in the past. We know that in Singapore many of the tradition-al substitutes or supplements for the family existed. There were peer organizations, particularly for unmarried women, and regional and surname organizations, as well as more formally organized clans. Some of the regional or surname organizations were primari-ly burial associations; but others provided various kinds of mutual support, such as credit unions. A few even sponsored schools. Some of the elders without family who wanted more personal ties devel-oped adoptive or *kai* relationships with younger persons who could provide care for them in their old age.

Wolf (1972) describes some of the socialization patterns of elder-ly women in villages of Taiwan in the 1960s. Hsieh (1984) gives a more recent picture of socialization of both men and women in a rural village. The government sponsored "Senior Citizen's Club" (sometimes called a "Long-Life Club") provided a peer group for men, and the Classroom for Mothers (Mothers' Class) included some elderly women. Informal social groups were more important in this particular village, however. There was an "old man's tea" group that met every morning at the home of one of the more affluent members, and small informal groups of elderly women gathered in the late afternoon at the pavilion of the village temple. Older women also gathered as neighborhood child-watching groups, supervising their grandchildren as they talked together.

Housing patterns in the city, however, discourage traditional forms of family and community life. They make it difficult for extended families to live together and encourage the development of nuclear families. A 1981 study of family patterns in Taiwan showed that of a sample of 1,040 households more than half (587) were "nuclear," 279 were "stem" (a couple living with unmarried children and the parents of either the husband or the wife), and 174 were "extended" (two or more closely related nuclear families living together and sharing common property) (Wong, 1981). Until recent years, housing policies in Singapore, increased the break-up of extended families and the movement toward nuclear family housing patterns. The Prime Minister's 1982 speech for Chinese New Year reported that nuclear families constituted 78% of the total number of families. He also reported that in 1980 there were 7,800 couples over the age of fifty living alone and almost 6,000 widows and widowers living alone.

Family income obviously influences the kinds of flats and houses that people can buy in Taiwan and Singapore and where they are located. In Taiwan, there has been greater freedom of choice, and family members have usually tried to find housing close to other family members, if they could not live together.

The natural kinds of community that are found in the rural areas do not exist in the city. Elders may have little opportunity to meet other elders. Older women may meet other women in connection with their child care or shopping activities outside the home. Men may meet other men in the parks or coffee houses (as noted in the Singapore Survey data). We were impressed with the socialization among men that occurred around tea drinking in the activity centers in Taiwan. Much is left to the initiative of the individual person, however, as to the quantity and quality of his or her social contacts; and there is traditionally a reluctance to associate with strangers. In Singapore, the different dialects spoken by older persons may make socialization difficult when other persons who speak the same dialect are not readily available. The groups sponsored by the government, churches, temples, or voluntary associations provide substitutes for some of the forms of community life found in the villages. The "void decks" are a natural place for elders to meet in Singapore, but even there the individual older person has to exercise some initiative to establish significant peer relationships. And, for those elderly who are physically handicapped, have hearing or sight problems, or are infirm, going out of the house or flat to socialize may be difficult or impossible. The Singapore Committee on the Problems of the Aged recognized the importance of "good neighbour (sic.)" visitation programs to relieve the loneliness of the homebound elderly. The meal delivery programs they recommended also are important forms of social contact. The Committee also recommended day care centers. Since 1985 the first comprehensive health centers have been established, which include day care and recreational programs as well as medical services, and a wide variety of neighborhood "befriender" services have been developed with help from the Ministry of Community Development (Wee, 1987).

The development of various kinds of peer groups to meet some of the social and emotional needs of the elderly has proceeded in Taiwan and Singapore with minimal involvement of the government. The emphasis is on sponsorship of organizations and activities by private groups, or when government social workers are involved, on involvement of the elders themselves in developing and conducting programs. Such an emphasis on concern for other persons and volunteer activity, which includes concern for persons outside the family, is somewhat alien to Chinese culture. Chinese values have focused on the family and on the family model as the basis for organizing community life at all levels. Such a model does not usually include the "stranger." City life, on the other hand, requires various kinds of contact with "strangers." The kinds of cohort organizations and relationships that are being promoted in Taiwan and Singapore are increasingly important to meet some of the social and emotional needs of older persons, but such development requires helping elders to overcome their ambivalence about "strangers," to develop a sense of "social welfare" beyond the family, and to appreciate the meaning and value of volunteerism. We have little evidence of how education is taking place for these purposes, but we were impressed with what we saw happening at the Populorum Progessio Institute in Taichung.

Natural opportunities for socialization with peers tend to occur in community. The reports on village life by Hsieh (1984) and Wolf (1972) emphasized the informal social groups of elderly men and women. Retired men found various kinds of opportunities to meet with each other informally. The lives of women did not tend to change much when their husbands retired, but much of the work of women was carried on out of the house, and women of various ages found frequent occasions to talk with their friends and neighbors. In the cities and suburbs, such opportunities are much more limited. Families live in much greater isolation from their neighbors, and the sheer number of families living in one area works against natural forms of community. Churches, temples, the "long life clubs," activity and community centers, and voluntary associations of various kinds offer some opportunities for community life, but the loneliness and isolation of many elders in the city is intensified by the lack of natural forms of community. This may be particularly painful for those who grew up in rural villages and had easy access to various forms of community life. The emphasis on community development coming from the Provincial government in Taiwan and the recommendations concerning community activities by the Committee on the Problems of the Aged in Singapore are important; but the task in the cities and suburbs is difficult, as life in cities in many other parts of the world demonstrates.

The socialization of the elders in Taiwan and Singapore continues to be focused primarily in the family, but changing family lifestyles make other resources for meeting social and emotional needs increasingly important. Little attention has been given to the remarriage of older persons after a spouse has died. The traditional Chinese family patterns discouraged such a practice; but the increasing numbers of isolated elderly and their continuing needs for physical contact, warmth, and closeness may make changes in the traditional patterns necessary.

As we noted in discussing family financial support, there are and will be increasing numbers of "survivors" who outlive both family and peer support groups. Their social needs will continue to be real, and they may not choose or need to live in some kind of institution. This is a particular group of elders who need to be considered in social planning.

VALIDATION

Old people, like all other people, need a sense of personal worth. It is one of the needs that is originally met (or not met) in the family. This is true in many cultures, but the Chinese context is very different from the American. The worth or "face" of the family was a primary value in the traditional Chinese context and the worth of the individual was seen in terms of his or her "place" in the family. "Place" had to do with the status, role, and functions of the individual member in the life and work of the family. "Place" was defined by the kinship system and symbolized by the "place" name given to the family member (older brother, younger sister, etc.). Secondarily, "place" might have to do with the status, role, and functions of a family member in the community, but "place" in the community was also viewed in terms of what it did for the family.

As we have seen, the "place" of the older members of the family in cities like Taipei, Taichung, and Singapore is becoming increasingly problematic. The data of our interviews in Taiwan and the National Survey in Singapore suggested that elders continue to be important members of their families. They are respected both in the family and the society, but their roles, functions, and authority are changing; and how long they will continue to be respected by the younger generations is a difficult question.

There are many reasons for the changes in the "place" of older persons in the family and community. Societies that are emphasizing rapid scientific and technological advances and the development of impersonal economic systems do not tend to have much respect for the past and for those persons who can no longer contribute to economic progress. There is less and less appreciation for what older persons have to offer. Inevitably such attitudes affect the young. The distance between the generations is increased if they speak different languages or dialects, as in Singapore, and if the older members of the family seem to be hanging on to beliefs, attitudes, and values that are very different from those of the young. The activities and diversions of city life leave little time or opportunity for the kind of communication between the generations that might close the gap.

Our informants in Taiwan and Singapore were aware of these problems. They emphasized the importance of good health for the elderly to be able to continue to perform important functions in family and community. They described, and we observed, both public and private efforts to provide resources for socialization outside the home that offer activities as well as sources of status and worth. But the primary concerns continue to be the role, status, and functions of elders in the family and the continuing influence of traditional ethical principles such reciprocity between young and old, filial piety, and respect for elders.

There are public efforts to encourage respect for the elderly. The city of Taipei annually celebrates "double nine day" (September 9) as a time to honor older citizens (age seventy and above) and to present them with gifts. Some of the elders with whom we spoke expressed concern, however, about changing attitudes and practices of "filial piety." There was also much concern in the public press. Editorials in the English language Taiwan newspaper spoke of the importance of "moral training" in the schools and Confucian understandings of moral behavior (see for example, an editorial in *The China Post* for July 29, 1985). Similar editorials were found in Singapore. The Singapore Prime Minister's 1982 New Year's Address put a strong emphasis on traditional Chinese moral values; and the Committee on the Problems of the Aged stressed the importance of moral education, particularly education in filial piety and respect for parents. Such education, their report said, must begin in the home. Filial piety must be taught by example. In addition to urging moral education in the schools, the Committee specifically recommended that newly married couples be required to participate in a program of family life education that focused on the responsibilities of family members for each other. The Committee did not see many problems in the relations of the present generation of elders to their children, but they expressed concern about what the situation may be when persons born after 1947 retire. Their *Report* says:

> . . . when they are due for retirement in 2010 and thereafter, they cannot be sure that their sons and daughters, who then would have families of their own, will take care of them in times of need. This is so, because, being born in the 1960s and 1970s, their bonds with Asian family-oriented moral values of filial piety and respect and reverence for the elderly are weak and would have been eroded by the influence of Western values of individualism and materialism. The care providers will probably be out working full-time. In any case, with successful family planning, there will be fewer sons and daughters to be care providers in the home. Therefore, the young must now be educated to make up for their smaller number with greater qualitative care. (p. 15)

The concern about filial piety and respect for the elderly affects every aspect of the relations between the generations, as the *Report* suggests, including the validation of the place of elders in the family. More than education may be needed, however, because the problem involves actual changes in roles and functions of the older members in family life and basic changes in the culture and the nature and purposes of family life. In the families that we observed in Taiwan, the place of the elder was clear when the elder was an important contributing member to the family as an economic unit–on the family farm or in the family shop. The place of the elder was also clear when he or she (usually she) was providing essential child care functions. When the contributions of the elder were no longer essential to the economic welfare of the family, what validated the place of the elder in the family was no longer clear or concrete and was much more dependent upon the feelings and attitudes of other family members and on the elder's own sense of worth. In fact, the elder might be actively seeking some kind of validation outside the family. The authority of the elder in a three-generation family, when the family housing does not belong to the elder and he, she (or they) are not contributing to the family income, is also no longer clear.

Ikels (1984) notes seven criteria developed by Rosow (1965, pp. 21-22) which have been important for the traditional "place" of elders:

1. They own private property (or control it) on which younger people are dependent.
2. Their experience gives them a vital command or monopoly of strategic knowledge of the culture, especially in preliterate societies.
3. They are links to the past in tradition-oriented societies, especially when they are crucial links to the gods in cultures with ancestor worship.
4. Kinship and the extended family are central to the social organization of the society.
5. The population clusters in relatively small, stable communities (gemeinschaft societies).
6. The productivity of the economy is low and approaches the ragged edge of starvation.
7. There is high mutual dependence among members of a group (pp. 11,12).

As Ikels points out, all seven of these criteria were met in traditional China. To what extent they are met in modern Taiwan and Singapore might vary somewhat from community to community and family to family, but the extent to which they apply to the elders in the cities with which we are familiar would be questionable.

Studies of village life in Taiwan gave us glimpses of the changing status, roles, and functions of retired farmers and fishermen. The men Hsieh (1984) interviewed in a farm village agreed that they had higher status than when they were young, but only as they were able to control a significant portion of the family's property after division. Older women continued their roles and functions in their homes, except for a few who had to continue to work for wages to support themselves or their husbands. Chang's study of a fishing village (1984) noted that retired men could retain little or no property of their own, but they continued to have positions of some authority:

> . . . although the younger generation already enjoys greater powers of self-determination . . . than in the past, the family head, or the senior parents, still retain important decision-making powers, especially with regard to major family decisions. (p. 5)

Wolf (1972) describes some of the important functions of an elderly woman in a village family under the conditions of the early 1970s:

> As long as an older woman retains her health and a fair degree of strength, she is an asset to a busy family. When her daughter-in-law's confinement leaves the household shorthanded, she can step in at a minute's notice, picking up familiar routines and running the family as smoothly as she did in years past. Family weddings, major birthdays, funerals, and large religious festivals are events that require a lot of woman power and a good deal of experience. They are considerably easier for the younger woman to handle if she can draw on her mother-in-law's memory of how things were done last time, or, as frequently happens, if she can hand the management of an event over to her mother-in-law completely. If the special event happens to be in the daughter-in-law's natal family, she enjoys it much more when she can leave all but her youngest child home with her mother-in-law and not have to rush back to put the evening meal on the table. For many a woman in her sixties, this lingering responsibility, the recognition by her sons and daughters-in-law of her continued competence, is a source of great satisfaction. (p. 222)

The division of farm families and the migration from the farms to the cities has continued at a rapid pace since 1970; and increasingly, as we have seen, the elderly parents (or parent) are left in the village to manage on their own, to move to live permanently with one of their children to live in a city, or to rotate from the home of one child to another on a regular basis. Wolf (1972) notes how difficult the "meal-rotation" system can be for the sense of worth of the elderly parents, particularly the elderly woman if the relationship with a daughter-in-law is difficult.

It was clear in our interviews in two cities of Taiwan that a high proportion (three-fourths) of our interviewees were seeking and finding sources of validation outside the family. They were finding new roles and functions and new sources of status in groups and activities that did not depend on home and family. And there was a small minority (two, in our sample) who had developed an individualistic way of living that deemphasized relationships, roles, and functions in the family. This data reflect the nature of our sample, and may not be typical. The data we have from Singapore suggest decreasing significance of the roles and functions of the older members in the family and declining authority, but tell us little about their sense of place. The male-oriented *Report of the Committee on the Problems of the Aged* gives considerable emphasis to older persons continuing in full-time or part-time employment. There may be an underlying assumption here that, for men at least, work outside the home is an important source of validation. Chinese culture is work-oriented and values the industriousness of the individual and society. We do not have evidence from our interviews or readings that leaving the work force created uncertainty about a person's worth, but we do have evidence from other experience that inability to do meaningful work can be a serious blow to self-esteem. How individual persons adjust to retirement is an important issue. We will discuss some aspects of this issue in the next section.

SELF AND WORLD TRANSCENDENCE

Sources of Meaning and Purpose for Life

The changing patterns of family life in Taiwan and Singapore not only create problems about the place of the older members, they also create problems about the meaning of life itself.

A person's sense of worth is not only influenced by experiences of role, status, and function in family and community context but also by experiences of values that transcend particular times, places, and relationships. Life may not have been as hard for the elders we interviewed in Taiwan as it had been for their parents and grandparents, but inevitably they had known some kind of hardship, pain, and suffering, and they looked for some kind of meaning and purpose that made it all worthwhile.

For some of our interviewees, this meaning and purpose was found in religious faith and activity and relationships in church or temple. For the most politically active man it was found in his vision of a united China. For a woman who had suffered a painful separation from her children in China, it was found in artistic creation and concern for handicapped students. Some had found a new source of meaning and purpose in "social welfare" and volunteer activity. For others, the focus of the meaning and purpose of their lives continued to be their relationships to family; and what came through from most of them was the underlying sense of the meaning of life as tied to family, both as a present reality and as an ongoing entity through the generations, with their grandchildren representing that continuity going on into the future.

The sense of meaningful continuity was difficult for some. The continuity with the past generations of their family had been broken by the exodus from the Mainland to Taiwan. The continuity with the future generations was stretched far across the ocean to the United States or Canada where the grandchildren resided, or where they hoped grandchildren would go for the completion of their education (and probably not return to Taiwan).

There was a difference, of course, between the Mainlanders and the Taiwanese. The Taiwanese had a stronger sense of the past and future of their own family; but here, too, the continuity had been broken by the Japanese occupation; and projection of family continuity into the future was difficult because of uncertainty about the future status of Taiwan as an independent nation.

There were also class differences in the values involved in family continuity. These were primarily differences in the value placed by some on education for the future of the family and by others on "good jobs" and the acquisition of material possessions. These differences seemed to be differences between "middle class" and "working class" elders. They seemed to be differences between tangible and immediate and intangible and long-range sources of family status and welfare.

The most serious problems that we found with family continuity as a source of the meaning and purpose of life were with farm families. Our sample was very small, but we observed that as families split and members moved to the cities important links between the generations tended to be broken. Family solidarity was no longer to be seen in an extended family living together under one roof. Family continuity was no longer focused on land that passed from one generation to another. Family authority was no longer located in the elders. The grandparents with whom we spoke said that their grandchildren would choose what they want to do (as their parents had done). The older generation no longer had any real influence over the important choices that children and grandchildren might make, a concern also for elders whose children and grandchildren lived in the United States or Canada. We also heard questions about the links between the generations in the family shop, when the older members talked of the splitting of the family and their uncertainty as to whether the next generation would want to continue the family business.

Of course, the reality was that in the rapid development of large businesses and industries, more and more of the younger generation were taking jobs that might produce income for the family but had little to do with family enterprises. Younger members found jobs appropriate for their education and experience rather than staying with the family farm or business. And as children established their families and had their own housing, income was primarily for their own families rather than for their families of origin.

It seemed clear in our interviews in Taiwan and our readings and discussions in Singapore that family identity continued to be important in ways that it is difficult for an American to understand, in spite of the radical cultural changes which are taking place. What we heard in Taiwan, however, was that it was becoming more and more difficult to focus much of the meaning of life on family continuity.

The Singapore Survey did not ask the kinds of questions that would speak to this concern, and there were important differences between the two countries that affected the meaning of family continuity; but both countries are very small and can be easily threatened by larger neighbors. The future of both countries is precarious. This uncertainty about the future was more in evidence in Taiwan. In Taiwan, it seemed that uncertainty about the future of the island as an independent nation was connected to some of the uncertainty about the future of the family. For our interviewees with children and grandchildren in the United States or Canada, however, family identity transcended national boundaries.

Just as individual identity has been tied to family identity in Chinese society; even so, the meaning of the life of the individual has been tied to the meaning of the life of the family. As family life changes, so the meaning of life changes. The present generation of elders and their children, according to the data we have from Taiwan and Singapore, seems to be holding to some of the traditional meanings of family in spite of the changes they have experienced. There is a real concern, expressed by many, about what will happen to the traditional values on which much of the meaning of life is based when the present and future generations of children establish their families.

Beyond the family, as we have noted, many of the people we talked with in Taiwan were finding meaning in service to others. This service was being performed as volunteers in activity centers, churches, and schools. Various kinds of service organizations which work with elders and enable elders to help each other were also in evidence in Singapore. "Social welfare" and "volunteerism" were relatively new to the Chinese, and there were many possibilities that were being developed. The elders who were learning the values of social service and the satisfactions of working as volunteers were healthy and active in their sixties for the most part. We wondered how many years they could continue this kind of activity and what would happen when they no longer had the interest, energy, or physical ability to go out of their homes to contribute their services as volunteers. We were also aware that the activities and services provided by community centers, "Long Life Clubs," "Evergreen

Academies,'' churches, and temples included only a small proportion of the elderly of the cities that they served and that there were limits to how long persons might participate in them.

There are other sources of meaning and value for life to be found in Chinese culture, of course, that help older persons find meaning for their own life and transcend their personal hardships. In Taiwan, there is the largest collection of Chinese art in the world. In the activity centers, we saw evidence of the interest of elders in the ancient arts of calligraphy and brush painting; and two of our interviewees, who no longer found meaning in family relationships, had found it in artistic creation. We also saw evidence of the interest of the elders in music, poetry, literature, and drama, and we learned that serving and drinking tea has esthetic as well as social meaning. The relationship with nature has been important in Chinese art and literature and in rural life. We observed elders in the parks of the cities and in the beautiful tourist areas such as Sun-Moon Lake and the East-West Highway through the mountains, but we did not have any direct evidence about relationship with nature as a source of meaning for elderly city dwellers in Taiwan and Singapore. We did, as we have noted, have some evidence of the importance of temples and churches as providing transcendent sources of meaning.

Superficial observation suggested that in both Taiwan and Singapore more and more emphasis was being placed on material things–housing, clothes, make-up and hair styles, cars, motorcycles, TV, audio and video cassettes, airconditioning, etc. The elders participated in this emphasis, although to a lesser extent than the younger generations. The acquisition of material possessions may be the outward and visible signs of a rising standard of living; but the question in our minds was whether, with the declining significance of the family and community and the loss of contact with the land and nature in both Taiwan and Singapore, the meaning of life was becoming increasingly materialistic; that is, focused more and more on economic success and material possessions.

Chapter Six

Individual Responses to a Changing Chinese Society (Taiwan)

INTRODUCTION

Our primary purpose in going to Taiwan was to learn as much as we could about the experience of individual Chinese elders in the changing situations with which they were being confronted. Our time was limited, and there was no way for us to contact a truly representative sample, but we wanted to learn as much as we could about the persons whom we were able to interview in order to put together a holistic picture of what the experience of aging was like for them. We supplemented our interviews with individual elders by speaking with a wide variety of resource persons and by making use of our readings and experience of Chinese culture.

In the previous chapter, we summarized the results of our study and our general impressions. In this chapter, we want to use the data from our interviews to put together stories of individual responses to the changing conditions of Chinese society in Taiwan. The stories contain only the "highlights" of what we learned in our interviews. The names and other identifying data of our interviewees have been changed to protect their identities, even though we obtained their permission to use data from their interviews in our report. The interviews were conducted in Taiwanese or Mandarin and were translated into English by our interpreter. Any direct quotes that we use are English translations of the responses of our interviewees as found in the notes that we made at the time of the interviews.

59

FROM FARM TO CITY:
A "GOOD LIFE"
FOR A WOMAN IN SPITE OF . . .

We visited with Mrs. Tsai in the home of her son in a suburban area. She was a woman in her late sixties who was living with her son and his wife, their two small children, and her invalid husband. Her son and his wife both worked, and so she had come to take care of the younger child when it was born. Earlier she had lived with an older son in another city until his children were grown. When we arrived, she welcomed us and waved her thin and limping husband into another room.

Her son had a three bedroom, one story, private house of his own; and living there was "comfortable," although somewhat crowded by American standards. Her son and his wife were both professionals, and their combined income provided adequately for the needs of the family. There was money for hired help to assist with housework and yard care. Two men were mowing the lawn outside with noisy mowers during our interview.

Mrs. Tsai spent her time caring for her husband and her grand-children. Her only activities outside the home were occasional visits to her other children and grandchildren and frequent visits on Sundays to friends in the village in which she grew up. She had five children, all living in Taiwan. She kept in touch with her other children by telephone "once or twice a month." She saw her sisters only once a year. Otherwise she talked with them "when something happens." When she traveled, she usually went by herself rather than depending on her son for transportation. On Sundays, when she visited her friends in the village, she went by bus.

When asked about her life, Mrs. Tsai told us first of her father, who was a farmer. Then she talked of her four brothers, who were also farmers, and of her four sisters, three of whom were still living. Mrs. Tsai was the seventh of nine children. She was married in her early twenties. Her husband developed a disabling condition after they had been married less than ten years. He had been disabled for thirty-seven years at the time of the interview. She said that he could walk with assistance but was deaf and had difficulty speaking. When her husband first became ill, neither his family nor her own could help Mrs. Tsai support herself, her husband and her children, and she had had to work very hard for the family to survive. She managed to keep the family together and to see that all the children were well educated. She was proud of her childrens' achievements. She felt that they respected and loved her very much because she had worked so hard for them.

Mrs. Tsai was raised in a Buddhist family, but she felt that Buddhism did not help her when she was having such a difficult struggle to care for her husband and support her family. She had been a Christian for a number of years. She said that the son with whom she was living was a Christian. She felt that God had been helpful to her in recent years but attributed most of her family's success to her own hard work. She was "too busy" most of the time to attend church.

When we asked what worried her, Mrs. Tsai responded that she had little to worry about. She and her family had a "good life." She said she was in "good health" and "didn't have time to be sick." She was concerned that life held so little for her husband, but she hoped that she would continue to be able to care for him and that she would not die before he did. She was not concerned about her own future. She said "It all depends on the gods; they will arrange it." Her hopes for her grandchildren were that they would have important jobs and a "good life." She believed it was important for them to study hard, graduate from college, and go on to graduate study in the United States or Canada. She said, "I will be angry if my grandchildren do not want to study."

FROM FARM TO CITY: A MAN CONTINUING TO LEARN. . . .

We visited with Mr. Lee in the tea room of a large activity center for elders where he worked as a volunteer. While we talked, he made tea for us in Taiwanese style; and we drank tea from little clay cups while we talked. Mr. Lee was a man in his mid-sixties who had been retired from teaching for thirteen years. He had been married for forty-four years and had seven children–two boys and five girls. He lived with his wife and his ninety-year-old mother in the same house in which he had lived for forty-one years. His oldest son lived in Canada and his second son lived in another city in Taiwan. Four of his daughters lived in Taipei, but one daughter lived in another part of the country. Mr. Lee had eleven grandchildren, two of whom lived in Canada. His son in Canada had returned to Taiwan only once for a visit, but he talked with him by telephone every two months.

When we asked about his life, Mr. Lee told us that he had grown up on a farm. His marriage had been arranged by his parents. His family had supported his leaving the farm and continuing his education. He was a university graduate. He also had studied in Japan. When he returned from Japan, he worked for the Weather Bureau for seven years. Then he began teaching at a vocational school of agriculture and had continued there until his retirement thirteen years ago. When he retired, he chose to receive his pension as a lump sum from the government. He lived on the income from his pension, supplemented by money that each of his children sent to him. He was the primary support for his elderly mother, who was cared for by his wife, although his younger sister had provided some care for her.

His children and grandchildren were a source of great pride to Mr. Lee. He talked fondly of visits to Taipei and family meals in a large restaurant with his children and grandchildren filling many tables. He believed that his children had done well, particularly the son in Canada. He described his family as having "no religion."

Mr. Lee said that he came to the activity center almost every day. The Director of the Center, whom we had met, had been one of his former students. He said that he was learning about "social welfare" from this former student. When we asked about his work at the center, Mr. Lee explained that the Bureau of Social Affairs in the city had made a list of all the retired people and then had mailed invitations to some of them to be "honor workers" in an activity center. As a retired teacher, he was helping in this center to organize courses for elders. He described courses in Chinese conversation, English conversation, basic English, calligraphy, Chinese painting, and Chinese music. When we asked if his wife participated in any of the activities at the center, he reminded us that his wife was at home caring for his mother.

TWO FARM FAMILIES: AN ENDANGERED SPECIES

In a suburb that had once been a farm village, we stopped in a bakery to talk with Mr. Hsu. He was a man in his early sixties who had left the family farm nine years before to help in the bakery owned by his eldest son. He said that "being a farmer is hard work." He and his two brothers had lived on the farm, but he and one brother had left the farm in the care of their other brother. Mr. Hsu now lived near the bakery with two of his younger sons and their children in a big house. His eldest son and his wife lived nearby with their five children–four sons and one daughter. During the day Mr. Hsu worked in the bakery, which was open from 7:00 a.m. to midnight seven days a week. Other family members took turns working in the bakery so that he could have a rest. His wife came to the bakery most afternoons. Mr. Hsu said that his daily schedule was to get up at 5:00 a.m., do exercises, work in the bakery, have lunch, take a nap, sit or visit in the bakery until dinner, and after dinner, watch television until it was time to go to bed.

Mr. Hsu usually visited his brother on the farm two or three times a month and then visited with friends in the farm village in which he had lived for many years; but he said that his friends were all old now and had grandchildren to care for. There wasn't much time for them to see one another. They did get together at weddings and funerals and other special occasions.

Mr. Hsu's elderly parents were still alive and lived a month at a time with each of the three brothers (the "meal rotation" system, or in Mr. Hsu's description, "eating around"). This month they were living with Mr. Hsu and his wife. His father was eighty-four years old and completely deaf. His father came to the bakery while we were there. Mr. Hsu said that his mother often came with his wife to the bakery in the afternoon. He told us that his parents spent most of their time walking around the "village" and sleeping. While we were at the bakery, five grandchildren also came, and we had the experience of seeing three of the four generations who were living together at that time. We did not meet the grandchildrens' parents. As we left, the five children were gleefully sharing three shiny bicycles, taking turns giving rides to the youngest, who rode on the handlebars.

When we asked Mr. Hsu what his hopes were for his grandchildren, he said that he hoped that they would do something "useful" and be independent, but he shrugged and said that he could not control what they would do. They would "be themselves" and do what they wanted to do.

* * *

We heard a similar message when we visited Mrs. Wu and her son on a farm a few hundred yards behind the two and three story shops and flats on a busy street. The farm had been in the family for two generations, but two of three sons had moved into the city. All three sons had jobs in the city. Each son farmed a third of the land, growing rice in their spare time. The family also included three sisters who were married and lived in the suburbs of the city. As a family farm, the land belonged to the deceased father's family. One of the father's brothers was still living, and the farm could not be divided or sold as long as the uncle was alive.

Living in the typical Taiwanese farm house were Mrs. Wu, age 73, her son, age 48, his wife, and three children–two sons and a daughter. The house was a long low building that had enough sleeping rooms for the three brothers and their families, who had all lived there earlier. It was made of brick and had a cement floor and a tile roof. The son's wife worked during the day, and so Mrs. Wu had cooked for the family, mended clothes, and taken care of the vegetable garden as long as she was able; but she did not appear to be in good health. When we arrived, she was sitting in her own small room. Her cooking hearth showed no signs of recent use. Mrs. Wu was concerned about her vision and her teeth. She did not have much hope that her vision would improve.

There was evidence that the family had begun to divide before the other two sons had moved out. Instead of the traditional one kitchen and one stove, there were three kitchen areas connected to three sleeping rooms. Each kitchen area had its own stove. The reception hall, which was the central room of the long, low building, was somewhat traditional. There was a Buddhist altar table against the center of the back wall. The picture of the deceased grandfather was on one wall. The room also served as the family

Homer L. Jernigan and Margaret B. Jernigan 65

dining area and had a refrigerator and a Chinese round "steamer" as well as a lacquered table and benches.

Mrs. Wu had grown up on a farm near the mountains. Her father worked on a tea plantation. Under the Japanese occupation, he had worked for low wages, which Mrs. Wu felt was "not fair." After the Japanese left, he leased land from the owner. With the land reform under Chiang Kai-Shek, her father was able to have land of his own, but Mrs. Wu said a "farmer's life was very hard." Life on the farm was all she had known; and the current price of rice was "not good," which added to the difficulties of life on the farm. Mrs. Wu expressed satisfaction with her life with her son and his family, however. She said she was happy with all her sons and her grandchildren, but her grandchildren were still too young for her to have any hopes for them. (Our impression was that Mrs. Wu was somewhat depressed.)

Mrs. Wu's son said that his children would make their own decision about whether they wanted to work on the farm. If they did not want to be farmers, he and his brothers would sell the land after their uncle's death.

THE FAMILY SHOP:
ANOTHER CHANGING TRADITION . . .

We visited with Mrs. Chin in a small camera shop owned by her eldest son. The shop was on a busy city street crowded with many other small shops. Mrs. Chin was an 81-year-old woman who worked as the cashier in the shop and lived with her son and his wife in an apartment on the second floor of the "shop house." We arrived in the morning before the shop opened. The windows of the shop were still covered with heavy metal grates. After the shop opened, we talked with Mrs. Chin while there was not much business. She sat behind the cash register as she talked with us. The shop was long and narrow, much of it being occupied by a Japanese machine that developed film while the customers waited. The shelves on one wall held cameras, film, and camera supplies. There was a Buddhist altar in a remote part of the shop. Mrs. Chin's eldest son ran the shop, and there was a total of five employees.

Mrs. Chin told us that she had grown up on a farm with six younger brothers and four younger sisters. Her parents had both lived long lives. Her father had been 95 when he died and her mother 85. One uncle had lived to be 99. She herself had three daughters and three sons, twenty-five grandchildren, and five great grandchildren. Some of her grandchildren and great grandchildren lived in the United States and Canada. Her husband had died thirty years earlier, and she had lived with her children since that time. She had been living and working with her eldest son for the last twelve years. She said that she was sad when her husband died, but she had good children who treated her with "filial piety." She had another son in the same city who came to see her two or three times a week, and she saw his children two or three times a month. She saw her son in Taipei only two or three times a year and his children only once every two or three years, but she kept in touch by telephone. She hoped that her grandchildren would have money and good health.

We also talked with Mrs. Chin's son, who was 60 years old, when he had a few spare minutes. He said that it was his responsibility to take care of his mother, but in this "new time" he wondered whether his children would take care of him when he was old. Perhaps he would just live with his wife after he retired. Ordinarily, the shop was open every day, but he was beginning to feel tired of working and was thinking of closing the shop in order to have a rest and take a tour "all over the world." He did not know whether any of his children would want to keep the shop going, and he said that his grandchildren in the United States were "more American than Chinese." His wishes for his grandchildren were that they "would study harder, go to a university, and take a major."

* * *

We saw a modern version of the family shop tradition when we visited with Mrs. Lim, a 76 year old widow, in the bakery and food store that she ran. Her store was one of three run by her family. Her son had a similar store on another street, and a grandson and his wife ran a third store. The store that we visited was large and modern, by Taiwan standards, and business was very brisk. Mrs. Lim said that there were twenty employees. The store was open from 7:30 a.m. to 10:00 p.m. every day. Mrs. Lim spent most of her time at the cash register and was there every day. She said that her work in the store had been important in order to support her family and to educate her children and grandchildren, and she could not give up working. She took one day off each month, leaving her daughter-in-law in charge.

Mrs. Lim had grown up in the city. She told us of one sister, who had five sons living in Taiwan, and a brother who had eight children, all of whom had emigrated to the United States. Mrs. Lim said that she had gone to school during the Japanese occupation and had had to study Japanese. A marriage was arranged by her parents. Her husband had owned two stores that sold glasses and watches, but he had died thirty years ago. When her husband died, Mrs. Lim did not receive any help from her husband's family or her own. She sold his stores and opened her own store, which she still continues to manage. She worked very hard, provided care for her children, and made sure that they were well educated. She contributed to the education of her grandchildren and was proud that all of them had graduated from the university. She had five grandchildren in Taiwan and three in the United States, where her daughter lived. She also had three great grandchildren. At the time we talked with her, Mrs. Lim was living with her daughter-in-law, the widow of one of her sons, who helped her in the store.

Mrs. Lim's life centered around the store and her family. She was a Buddhist, but she seldom went to the temple. Many of her customers were also her friends. She appeared to be in good health. She told us that she had exercised regularly every morning for thirty years, but recently she had stopped as "it no longer felt good." She left the store for awhile almost every day to walk to the market and to go to the apartment above the store for a two hour nap. She kept in close touch with her son and grandson who operated the other two family stores, but she said little about times with other family members.

When we asked what she had learned from her life experience, Mrs. Lim responded that what was most important was good education for children. She also emphasized musical ability and competence in English conversation. She wanted all of her children and grandchildren to have good health, to be "good boys and girls," and to make money. She said they would choose their own jobs, and she could not choose for them. If they wanted to run a store, it would be hard work and keep them very busy. She said she did not have any wishes for herself for the future, only wishes for her children and grandchildren to have good health and a useful life.

A "MAINLANDER" GROWING OLD AS A CHRISTIAN IN A NON-CHRISTIAN COUNTRY . . .

Mr. Chang volunteered to meet us at the YMCA where we were staying. We sat around a table in the dining room as we talked with him. He was a 78-year-old retired pharmacist who had come from the Mainland in 1949 with Chiang Kai-Shek's army. He had worked in the pharmacies of military hospitals in Manchuria, Peking, Nanking, and then Taiwan for twenty years. He had retired at the age of fifty-eight and accepted a lump sum payment from the government.

Mr. Chang had been much involved in Christian churches and in church-related activities since his retirement. He had worked as secretary of a mission church until the missionary in charge claimed the church property as his own. The church in which he was currently involved had also lost its building but was now self-supporting and was working toward obtaining a new building. He had served as pastor of the church for awhile. He had also taught a weekly Bible class in Mandarin at a Childrens' Home until he was seventy-five. Currently he was doing some volunteer work in a "mission community," and he also visited occasionally in an "old peoples' home." When he was not doing volunteer work, he liked to walk in the park and stop to talk with people. He said that some of the people with whom he talked became Christians. He also said that he thought that too many old people were sitting in the park with nothing to do. He did not like to waste time.

Mr. Chang's mother and sister had been Christians in Mainland China. His father had had "no religion," but he remembers his parents teaching him about Confucius. His parents had arranged a marriage for him when he was in high school. He went on to study pharmacy in the university and did not see his intended bride for seven years, but his marriage had lasted for fifty years. He described his wife as "very strong"; but now at age seventy-seven she had lost her memory. He and his wife had three sons. The oldest son had served in the army but had retired and was making fans. His oldest son had three daughters. The second son had been out of the country working as an engineer, but he and his family (three children) had returned to Taiwan and were living with Mr. Chang and his wife. The third son was also an engineer, living with his wife and two children in Africa.

Mr. Chang thought his health was good for his age. He believed that for good health it was important "to be happy, to work when you work; to play when you play." He said that he tried to walk for an hour each day. Happiness was important for health and also was helpful to others. He hoped to spend the rest of his life in happiness trying to help other people. He thought the most important thing for a Christian was to try to live according to the Bible; but it was hard to live that way and some people preached about living according to the Bible but did not do it. Life according to the Bible was a life of "love, joy, and peace" made possible by the power of the Spirit. A Christian was a "new creature" who had been "born again." His hope for his grandchildren was that they would be Christians.

A "MAINLANDER" WHO HAD DEVELOPED A NEW LIFESTYLE

We visited with Mrs. Wong in a modern duplex in the suburbs where she lived with her husband. She welcomed us warmly and was glad to tell us about her activities at the age of seventy-four. We soon learned that she was an artist who was glad to have us take pictures of some of her art work. Her current project was painting fans, which she expected to sell at a fair in the fall in order to raise money to help handicapped students at the university where her husband had been a professor for many years. Mrs. Wong showed us other examples of her paintings and her calligraphy. She tried to do some painting and calligraphy every day. She was also taking a course in calligraphy. We learned that Mrs. Wong enjoyed being a student as well as helping other students. She had taken many courses at the university, three or four each year, and expected to continue taking courses in many different fields. Her special interest at the university was the handicapped students, but she was also interested in helping students with their writing and painting. She was currently serving as a teacher in the painting club.

Mrs. Wong lived a very busy life. She arose early in the morning. She did housework and cooked for her husband, but her special interests were flowers and art. She spent as many hours as she could each day with her art work. She said there was never enough time, and she never felt lonely. She did take a nap each day after lunch. She defined herself as "student, wife, painter, calligrapher."

With some reluctance, Mrs. Wong told us about her family background on the Mainland and her current family. She seemed to prefer to talk about her current interests and activities. Mrs. Wong had been born in Northwest China. She had two brothers and a sister. Her father was an engineer. She described him as a "very open-minded" man who gave his children freedom to do as they liked. Mrs. Wong was the youngest child. She went to a university and became a teacher after graduation. Her father was a Christian, and she met the man who became her husband at a church conference one summer in Beijing. After the conference, she kept in touch with him by letter. Finally, a marriage was arranged. She and her husband had been married almost fifty years. He became a well-known scholar. When they left the Mainland for Taiwan, Mrs. Wong found a job as a newspaper editor and worked in this position for twenty-five years. She had been retired for ten years. Her husband was a Christian, but she said that she was "free of religion."

Mrs. Wong told us a little about her own family. She had a son who lived in the United States and a daughter who lived in another city. She had two grandchildren in the United States and one in Taiwan. She said her daughter was "very busy" and kept in touch by telephone. The only free time was during summer and winter vacations. Her impression was that relationships between parents and children were not as close as they used to be, and she thought that elders should have their own life and not be dependent on their children.

She did not identify herself as a religious person, but when asked what she thought was important in life, Mrs. Wong responded that the important things in life were "spiritual" and not "material." She believed that the biggest problem with the elderly was that "they do not know how to spend time–how to spend life." In her life, much of her time was spent "helping others."

(Our impression was that Mrs. Wong had developed an independent lifestyle that was very different from the other Chinese women we interviewed, but we sensed that there was something very painful about her family history that made her reluctant to talk about her children and grandchildren.)

* * *

The interviews we have described provide illustrations of differing reactions of individual persons to their own histories and to the changing conditions of Chinese society in Taiwan. There were other people who shared their stories with us. We enjoyed all of the interviews and wished we had time for more. The stories that we have presented briefly in this chapter show something of the variety of individual experiences and some of the common concerns that elders expressed as they were confronted with changing family situations. These individual stories provide glimpses of the human side of the generalizations that we included in the previous chapter about what we had learned in Taiwan and Singapore.

Chapter Seven

Interactions of Personality, Culture, and Religion in the Experience of Aging

The specific focus of our studies in Taiwan and Singapore was the experience of aging in Chinese society. This focus was part of our general interest in the interactions of personality, culture, and religion in the experience of aging in many different cultural contexts. As suggested in Chapter One, we did not try to identify "religion" as a separate aspect of the experience of aging. We tried to develop a "holistic" approach to the experience of aging that would include important elements of what is often defined as "religious" or "spiritual." We assumed that people age as "whole" persons and that, therefore, understanding and working with the elderly should involve understanding and working with "whole" persons. If there are "religious" or "spiritual" aspects of being a whole person, then those aspects should not be separated from other aspects of experience. We recognize the difficulties involved in definitions of "religious" and "spiritual" that relate to the concepts of particular "religions" or "faith groups." We have tried to identify aspects of the experience of aging that transcend particular cultures and particular definitions of "religion." With our students we have studied these aspects of the experience of aging in different ethnic groups; and in Taiwan and Singapore, we wanted to see what we could learn when we were able to do more intensive study of the experience of aging in one cultural context–Chinese society.

For purposes of review, we want to repeat the summary of the four aspects or "windows" on the experience of being a person which we included in Chapter One:

- the physical survival aspects, which have to do with a person's ability to cope with the necessities of human existence (food, clothing, shelter, income, health, sanitation, mobility, sleep, exercise, etc.);
- the relational aspects, which have to do with a person's ability to relate to other persons (one-to-one, family, peer groups, and various forms of social and communal relationships) not only for coping but also for various forms of emotional satisfaction, including "love";
- the validation aspects, which have to do with a person's sense of worth or self-esteem, or in Oriental terms, the sense of "place" or "face" in the family, community, and world;
- the self and world transcendence aspects, which have to do with a person's sense of the meaning and purpose of life, and the life commitments and relationships that facilitate adjustment to and transcendence of the day-to-day vicissitudes of life.

These aspects of individual experience interact with and are strongly influenced by the ways in which a particular culture:

- develops access to natural resources, information, tools, technologies, coping patterns, institutions, and systems that contribute to the survival of the individual and the culture;
- provides mutually supportive and need-satisfying forms of social interaction (socialization);
- defines the status, role, and functions of the individual in the light of the culture's values and priorities and enables the individual to experience a sense of personal worth and significance;
- develops collective sources of meaning and purpose for life in which individuals can participate and which, to some extent, they can internalize through participation in the myths, symbols, and rituals of the culture and/or some form of its religious heritage.

As we reflect on the questions we asked of our interviewees and our resource persons and the answers that we received, we have a clearer sense of what we mean by interactions of personality, culture, and religion in the experience of aging. We have a sense of the interweaving of the various aspects of personal and cultural experience in the total experience of being an elderly human being. We also have an increasing appreciation of the complexity of the experience of aging in modern society. We want now to look at the interweavings of the different aspects of personal and cultural experience that we saw by examining the information and impressions that we gathered in Taiwan and Singapore. We will use the four different aspects of personhood as headings under which to organize these interweavings.

PHYSICAL SURVIVAL

As we asked about the "physical survival" aspects of experience, we were asking what helped a person to cope with basic needs for food, clothing, shelter, sleep, exercise, etc. The answers came not only in terms of the struggle to provide income and other resources to meet those needs but also in terms of meanings and values. For our Chinese elders, their efforts not only provided income, housing, food, etc., to help their families but also contributed to their families' quality of life and helped to provide what they thought was most important for their children and grandchildren (the most common example being education). The struggle was more than a struggle for the necessities of life; it was a struggle to fulfill the roles and functions of elders in their families in the past, the present, and the future in spite of radical changes in circumstances. It was a struggle to realize values that gave life meaning and purpose in a changing society.

When we asked the elders with whom we talked what had been helpful when times were hard, we were asking not only where material resources came from but also where the elders had found strength for coping in spite of all the obstacles and difficulties. The answers varied. Some had found strength in their religion. Some had found strength in themselves (e.g., the kind of self-confidence that might be found in traditional humanistic Confucianism). Some believed that their own "hard work" had been the key. Some had relied primarily on family relationships and resources. All the answers reflected dependence on something beyond the immediate situation, on some kind of "faith" or trust based on previous experience and previous learning that had proved to be dependable in times of adversity.

Beyond personal resources for coping, the resources available in the culture were important. In Chinese culture, the primary resource was and continues to be the family; but the ways families cope have been changing rapidly. The farm family worked together as an economic unit. The family shop was also an economic unit. The requirements for operating a successful family farm or shop strongly influenced the family lifestyle and the roles, functions, and status of the elderly members. But all that was changing as new technological developments made farming less labor intensive and opened up new opportunities for family members to work in businesses, industries, government, service agencies, etc. The family life that had been highly cohesive on the family farm and in the family shop was becoming increasingly fragmented. Elders spent more and more time separated from other family members and had less and less to do to contribute to the family welfare, especially when there was little or no need for child care at home.

In addition, the situation of the elders was, and is, increasingly tied to their financial resources. If they had no income of their own after the division of family property, they easily became dependent on the "meal rotation" system, which was a radical change in the role, status, and functions of elderly parents. Their situation might be better if they were able to live with one child and his or her family for their remaining years, but they were financially dependent on a family budget which was being stretched in more and more ways. In either situation, the quality of their lives was tied to the quality of their relationships with their children, their childrens' spouses, their grandchildren, and the degree to which the other members of the household honored the traditional values of reciprocity, filial piety, and respect for elders. Although traditionally elders could share in family income just as other members of the family, they needed income that they could spend on their own needs and interests, particularly in the city or suburbs where most activities and most of the necessities as well as the pleasures of life cost money. Moreover, our impression was that most of the elders with whom we talked felt better about their place in the family if they were able to make a contribution to the financial welfare of the family, either by contributing from their own income or from their labor, or both.

The increasing importance of material resources for families with a rising standard of living tended to put more emphasis on income, but the "spiritual" or ethical resources of the family continued to be strongly emphasized by our interviewees when they stressed the importance of "filial piety" in their lives. Again and again, however, we heard the concern about the ethical values of the younger generations who were becoming more individualistic and were subject to increasing influences of "Westernization." The obligations of children to support their parents are part of the Chinese cultural tradition; but when the ethical foundations of such traditions erode, external pressures may have little effect.

Our impressions were that, in spite of changing cultural patterns and values, families could, for the most part, be counted on to provide the basic needs of the elderly members. The interactions of the elders with the rest of the family around financial issues were increasingly important, however; and the changing attitudes of the younger generation toward the elders were of increasing concern.

There were certain needs, however, which could easily exceed the coping resources of the family. A family's financial resources, for example, might become more and more strained to support elderly members at the same time that expectations about family consumption were growing in line with general increases in the standard of living and the pressures to provide more educational opportunities for children and grandchildren. The most obvious limitations of family resources, however, might have to do with medical care, as we have noted earlier. Both the catastrophic and chronic illnesses to which elders are susceptible could quickly exhaust family resources. The problems of trying to care for a handicapped or bedridden elderly parent at home might place great stress not only on a family's financial resources but also on their own human resources as they tried to meet the demands of family survival and elder care at the same time.

Various kinds of resources provided by the surrounding community are becoming necessary to assist the family to care for sick or frail elderly at home. "Day care centers" for elders who are able to be out of the house during the day were, and are, being explored in both Taiwan and Singapore, but we heard of resistance on the part of elders to participation in such centers unless they provided some kind of physical therapy. Other resources to assist the family with the care of a sick or infirm member were also being developed.

Most of the elders with whom we talked, and most of those included in the Singapore survey, were living with family members. If they did not live with family members, they lived in reasonably close proximity to family members. Housing was not a major problem. But there was evidence that increasing numbers of elderly couples were living on their own, and there was increasing need for housing under both private and public auspices for elders to live on their own. Even those who lived with family members might be spending long hours each day on their own. One of the obvious questions, to which we did not have a clear answer, was how adequate the nutrition was for people living alone or spending much of each day alone. Another question, which we know is being addressed to some extent in Singapore, was the adequacy and safety of housing for elderly parents or grandparents in the highrise "flats" or apartment houses in which most people tend to live in the cities. We wonder about who should have the ethical responsibility for developing standards of safety and accessibility of housing for the elderly.

Some aspects of coping depend upon the elders' own choices or initiatives in making use of resources and opportunities provided by their society. They have some choice, for example, whether to make use of the free annual medical checkups available to them in Taiwan. One of our interviewees suggested that some "old people" do not choose to take advantage of the annual medical checkup because if they are feeling well they do not want to know whether they have any medical problems. Elders also have to exercise some initiative to make use of the free or reduced-rate transportation facilities available to them. They have some choices that they can make about their sleeping patterns, as noted in our individual interviews. They also have choices about what to do about exercise. Some of the traditional forms of exercise in Chinese culture are more than physical activities. They have philosophical and religious significance as well, but the evidence of the degree of participation in such activities by the participants in the Singapore Survey was not encouraging. The data of that study suggested that large numbers of elders, when not involved in housekeeping or childcare responsibilities, were spending much of their time at home in relatively passive forms of activities such as listening to the radio or watching television or video cassettes. Most of the persons we interviewed in Taiwan reported some form of regular exercise, but this may reflect the nature of our sample. Our interviewees did not talk of participating in traditional exercise programs.

The availability of resources in the culture that help elders to cope with the necessities of life and to meet some of their needs for socialization and validation is important. Without an effective system of informing and educating the older members of the population about such resources and their potential values, however, many elders may not take advantage of them. Members of an elderly population who look primarily to the family to meet their needs may not look for resources outside the family. Elders who have spent most of their lives in rural communities may find it difficult to trust or use the more impersonal resources of cities or suburbs. In the next section we will look at the question of what motivates elders to go outside of their homes to meet some of their needs.

The interactions of personality and culture in the experience of aging become very complex around the basic issues of physical survival. In Chinese society, as we have seen, much depends upon the interactions within the family system; but the resources of the surrounding culture are also important, as are the individual choices and initiatives of individual elders in making use of the resources available to them beyond the family.

SOCIALIZATION

One of the important questions about the choices and initiatives of Chinese elders in Taiwan and Singapore was the extent to which they looked beyond the family for relationships with people. The family as the primary focus of social relationships was clear in our interviews and in the Singapore Survey data. But the fragmentation of the family under the conditions of urban living has greatly reduced the quantity of social interaction in the family, if not the quality; and we saw evidence of reductions in quality as well, particularly between grandparents and grandchildren. The reports we had available concerning social life in rural villages emphasized the importance of informal groupings of men and women, as well as the more formal groups organized under government sponsorship. In the cities, there was less likelihood of informal groupings; and formal groups, such as the "Long-Life Clubs" and the activity centers, were more important as resources of socialization beyond the family and individual friendships. The initiative of elders to go outside the family and to choose to participate in such groups obviously had much to do with the experience of individual persons. In a family-oriented culture in which traditional forms of community life no longer exist, what motivates such initiative? Particularly, what motivates individuals not only to participate in such groups but to take responsibility for the activities and welfare of such groups? In a family- and community-oriented society, in which strangers are suspect, what motivates people not only to socialize with strangers but to serve them freely? In the activity centers, we noted that retired teachers or educators were continuing to teach or to take responsibility for program development. Some of them had become interested in "social welfare" through their exposure to religiously-oriented adult education programs. We know that some of the elders who were taking responsibility in activity centers responded to an invitation from the city to be "honor workers" (not "volunteers" because of the way that term had been abused during the Japanese occupation). The Christians with whom we talked were motivated to find social supports outside the family in churches and to participate in church activities and programs because of their religious commitments. Generally, however, it was not clear to us what motivated elders to participate in the clubs and the activity centers that are sponsored by the government.

In Singapore, opportunities for informal socialization occur on the "void decks," and the weather permits regular opportunities for interpersonal and group relationships out of doors. The community centers provide opportunities with more structure, as do churches and temples. A wide variety of voluntary agencies exists that both serves elders and involves them in service activities. When participation is left to individual initiative and choice in a Chinese society, the question of motivation arises, as we have observed. Under the conditions of urban life, the need for socialization outside the family is increasing all the time; but where is the motivation that helps to overcome traditional resistance to such socialization? The multiplicity of Chinese dialects spoken by the elderly in Singapore and their lack of education in Mandarin or English add additional difficulties to the possibilities of socialization outside of their own language groups.

Questions of individual initiative and choice cannot be asked in the same way in Chinese society as in the United States. Individuals, including individual elders, are participants in a family system; and the family becomes involved in such decision-making. The traditional orientation toward family encourages the older family members to focus their interests and activities in the home in spite of changing family circumstances. Family pressures, however, may be part of the answer to the question we are raising. Families may need to encourage older members to leave the apartment or "flat" and develop social contacts outside the family, or families may discourage such contacts; but the family is part of the decision process. Beyond the realities of individual and family needs, however, the issue of motivation seems to us to be a religious or ethical issue tied to the larger question of a redefinition of "the good life" for elders in Chinese society. When "the good life" for many centuries has emphasized relationships in the family and traditional forms of community, what new definitions of "the good life" for elders are needed to meet the changing conditions of life in both the village and the city?

VALIDATION

The issues around socialization and validation overlap. Validation in Chinese society involves the mutual interaction of the individual and significant others around role, status, and function, as we have noted. Love and affection may not be as important in Chinese society as in the West, but recognition and respect in terms of the individual's place in family and community (when and where community exists as a significant reality) are very important. The worth of the individual is measured primarily by his or her contribution to the welfare and reputation or "face" of the family. Individual pride is connected to family pride, and individual shame is connected to family shame.

Traditionally, the place of elders in the family was a place of respect regardless of the roles that they played or the functions they performed. They had authority by virtue of their position as elders, and younger family members were expected to respect their authority and to obey their dictates. The reality of this ideal place for elders in the traditional family may have varied in actual family life, but our impression is that this ideal place is seriously challenged by the changing situation in Taiwan and Singapore. The data and illustrations of the previous chapters provide glimpses of this challenge. The farmer or the fisherman and his wife who are reduced to living with their children in some kind of rotation system may be respected but have little real authority, especially if they have no property or income of their own. An elderly wife and mother may have little or no authority in the houses of her daughters-in-law or sons-in-law. Elderly parents living in the city with their children and grandchildren may have important functions of childcare when the grandchildren are small; but as the grandchildren move out into worlds of their own and the generation gap grows, respect and obedience to the grandparents may seriously diminish. The role of the elder on the family farm or in the family shop may continue to be important, both in terms of family income and family cohesion; but even here, as we have seen, the discontinuities between the generations may be more powerful than the continuities. Here, too, the status and authority of the elders is decreasing.

We have observed that participation in some kind of peer group is another source of validation for elders in Taiwan and Singapore. Status and respect may come with the role they play in such groups. At least, they may find friendship with persons with common interests and find activities to fill some of the hours of the day that otherwise might be lonely at home. In the churches and temples, such relationships may be more than social. They may have significance in terms of contributions to purposes that transcend the individual and the group. They may contribute to feelings of per-

sonal worth that are not dependent upon particular social relationships. Similarly, some of the elders with whom we talked, who did
not think of themselves as "religious," had social contexts in
which they continued to contribute to purposes that transcended
themselves and their families (e.g., the values of education or the
welfare of other people) or had found new ways to make such
contributions (e.g., continuing education for elders, creativity in
brush painting or calligraphy, "social welfare").

Apart from formal or informal peer groups, the experience of
significant interpersonal relationships outside the family and the
kind of mutual support and validation that is possible in such relationships can be an important part of a Chinese elder's life, as with
elders in other parts of the world. Such interpersonal relationships
are possible but more difficult in the city. As we have seen, problems of distance and transportation, may make it difficult to continue old friendships. And, as time goes by old friends may die or
become incapacitated. New friendships may be difficult to establish
in the city, and they may not even be desired. The loss of old relationships may also be a loss of important sources of validation; and
it may be difficult for the elder living a somewhat isolated life in
the village or city to find new sources to give him or her this validation.

In a few instances, such as the woman described in the last section of the previous chapter, we observed persons whose validation
was no longer tied to family, to friendships, or to participation in
particular groups. This woman had found interests in painting and
calligraphy that filled many hours of her schedule. Moreover, she
saw painting and calligraphy as a way of being helpful to other
people, both through the money these activities could bring, which
could be of help to handicapped students, and the teaching and
sharing she could do, which could help other people with similar
interests. She also had an interest in lifelong learning that motivated
her to continue to take courses in the university. She participated in
groups of various kinds, but her sense of place in life did not seem
to be dependent upon recognition and respect in those groups. She
was investing her time and energies in forms of creativity and learning that suited her talents and her interests, and she was contributing to various kinds of groups. We had the impression, however,

that she did not need the approval or recognition of particular groups. She would continue to invest herself in values that she thought were important and to find places to express those values. Other people were important, but groups might come and go (just as, for her, her family had come and gone).

In a somewhat similar way, the retired pharmacist who identified himself as a Christian, had worked with different churches, classes, and institutions, and continued to find ways to express his Christian faith even though the particular groups with which he was working might change. He, too, did not seem dependent on validation either by his family or by specific groups.

Both socialization and validation in the long run, however, tend to be dependent on two necessary conditions. The first is health. The persons whom we interviewed recognized that they were able to do what they did in family and/or group settings because they had reasonably good health. The second is money. Most of our interviewees did not have much money, but they had enough to do what they wanted. Some of them were continuing to work in individual or family enterprises and expected to do so as long as they were physically able because they played a part in providing for the family. Those who were retired felt secure enough about their family income and their family situation that they did not need to spend their time and energy contributing to family survival. Family needs were provided for, and they could afford to do other things. They also had resources to provide for their own needs, which meant that they could afford the clothes, the transportation, and the other necessities that went along with their activities outside the home.

As we think about the stages of the aging process, which we have observed in various cultural contexts, we think about the changes that may make contributions to family and community difficult. Failing health, chronic illness, or physical handicap may be among those changes. Sometimes these changes may involve the failing health, chronic illness, or physical handicap of another family member. Changing circumstances may also mean a serious reduction or loss of income. Many things can happen to interfere with the coping resources and the forms of socialization and validation that an individual elder or an elderly couple have known. What happens then to the sense of meaning and purpose for life that may be tied to an elder's ability to contribute to family or community?

Our experience working with individual persons in other cultural contexts has taught us that it is not only external sources of validation but also internal sources that may be important. Some persons may have internal sources which help them to maintain a sense of worth or "place" in spite of changing external circumstances. Other persons, out of their own personal history and problems in their internalized sources of validation, may have difficulty in having a secure sense of their place in family and community even though the external situation includes significant relationships with other persons and groups and appropriate recognition of their contributions to those relationships. Our impression is that Chinese elders may be less dependent upon psychological sources of status or worth than Americans of the same age, but we recognize the importance of psychological influences in both cultures. We also recognize the importance of finding sources of meaning and purpose for life for older persons in all cultures that are not dependent upon personal relationships and day-to-day activities and are not tied to the individual person's subjective feelings about life.

SELF AND WORLD TRANSCENDENCE

Some Concluding Questions

The question of sources of meaning and value for life that cannot be lost or taken away is the basic question of "self and world transcendence." It also may be the basic question raised by the experience of aging. It is a serious question for elderly in a society in which the traditional source of meaning and value for life has been focused on the family as a present reality of living persons and relationships, a past reality of ancestors, and a future possibility of children and grandchildren. We have discussed some of the changes that are influencing the meaning and significance of the family in Taiwan and Singapore. We have noted and illustrated some of the problems involved for elders who continue to see their place in the family as the primary source of the meaning and purpose for their lives. We have identified some of the sources of strength that elders have found in times of trouble, which may or may not have included the family and family resources. We have looked at other kinds of relationships and other ways in which elders are finding a sense of place or worth. We ask now the difficult question, "What do Chinese elders have that cannot be lost?" We ask, "What do the elders, whom we came to know, have that cannot be lost amid the changes that occur as they experience many different personal and social circumstances before they die?"

Some of the answers seem reasonably clear. Most of the elders we met have, and will continue to have, family as a major focus for the meaning and purpose of their lives. They belong to a generation that holds to the importance of family and the related virtues of reciprocity, filial piety, and respect for elders. They have raised children who, for the most part, have held to the same values, even though the circumstances are markedly different in which those children, now grown, are raising their families. But what about the new generations? We have noted that some of the elders whom we interviewed expressed their uncertainty about their grandchildren following the old ways and the old values. They have reason to doubt the continuities of the family tradition and the family values in the coming generations. And, as we have seen, these doubts were also expressed by some of the resource persons with whom we talked and some of the literature that we read.

We are also aware that there are those elders who, for one reason or another, have become separated from family or have survived after other members of their family have died. When they no longer have family, what happens to their sense of meaning and purpose for life?

We have looked at some of the other sources of meaning and purpose for life for elders beyond family. We have seen elders who were finding status, role, and functions in informal and formal groups of their peers. We have seen some concerned about "social welfare" and motivated to be of service to other people. We respect their investments in such sources of meaning and purpose that may be somewhat novel and strange in Chinese culture. We assume that some of them will be able to find ways to be of service and to contribute to the quality of life for others as long as they are physically able. We are concerned, however, about what happens if and when they are no longer physically able to engage in these kinds of activities or, if for some other reason, they have to terminate their service activities.

We have some of the same kind of concern about the Christians whom we interviewed. They had found a source of meaning and purpose for life in their relationship to God and the church, but sometimes that meaning and purpose tended to be tied to activities and contributions to church life. Is their relationship to God and their sense of being accepted and supported by the church strong enough to sustain them when they can no longer be active? We don't know the answer to that question either. In theory, we know the answer in terms of our understanding of the nature of the relationship to God and the church that is taught in Christian theology. We have enough experience in activity-oriented American churches, however, to know that theology may not make much difference to elders who experience the meaning and purpose of their lives as dependent on their abilities to contribute to the work of the church.

We talked with Buddhists and Confucianists and persons who had "no religion." We did not learn enough from the Buddhists to have any clear sense of how their Buddhism gave them a sense of meaning and purpose for life that transcended what was happening or might happen to their families or to themselves as individuals. They seemed as dependent on family for their sense of meaning and purpose as anyone else. We know, in theory, that Buddhism offers a way to transcend the pleasures and vicissitudes of this life, to experience enlightenment, and to escape the cycle of continuing reincarnations; but we did not hear much about how Buddhism and Buddhist worship were helpful in dealing with the changing circumstances of daily life.

The persons with Confucian backgrounds impressed us with their confidence in themselves and human nature. One man particularly was holding to a continuing hope that Confucian principles, as interpreted by Sun Yat Sen, father of the Chinese Republic, would some day be the basis for a unified China. A woman who said she had "no religion" was investing her life in her painting and calligraphy, continued learning and teaching, and service to handicapped students. She seemed to have a sense of mission or purpose for life that transcended family and particular human relationships. We wondered, however, what might happen if the time came that she could not engage in painting or calligraphy, go to classes, or do anything for handicapped students. What would she then find that would give her life meaning and purpose?

SELF AND WORLD TRANSCENDENCE: RELIGION AND SPIRITUALITY

What we have called "self and world transcendence" has to do with the way persons put their lives together around that which they have experienced as giving life meaning and purpose. It has to do with the organization of life around values that both transcend the day-to-day experiences of life and give those experiences meaning. "Self and world transcendence" has to do with that which makes life worth living in spite of all the hardships of human existence. As we have seen, organizing life around transcendent meanings and values cannot be separated from the other aspects of life that we have been discussing. Physical survival, social relationships, and validation are all interrelated and are all involved in how a person puts life together. And how a person puts life together is much influenced by the cultural context in which a person lives.

We have been talking about the experience of Chinese elders in a rapidly changing cultural context. We have emphasized the changing Chinese family and the difficulties for elders in Taiwan and Singapore in using the "symbol" or "myth" of family as the primary source of meaning and purpose for life. In a sense what we have been talking about is "religion." One of the traditional roots of the word "religion" is "religiare–to bind," and we have been talking about how Chinese elders "bind" life together. Talking with elders is particularly important because they have had many years of experience and they have been through many different kinds of situations. How, then, do they "bind" life together in terms of what life means to them in the face of all that they have been through? We do not pretend to have talked enough with each individual to have definitive answers to that question, but we do have our impressions based on what we were able to ask.

We have also raised a normative question that seems inevitable in the light of the vicissitudes of the aging process–What sources of meaning and purpose for life do elders have that cannot be lost in the face of the changing realities they may have to face? This may be interpreted to be the question of "spirituality"–the question of the meanings and values or the "center" (or "centers") around which life is bound together. We have looked at various sources of meaning and value that we learned from Chinese elders in the light of this question of what cannot be lost. We have not tried to evaluate one form of "spirituality" or one "center" in relation to other forms of "spirituality" or other "centers" around which life is organized. We have raised the "spiritual" question of the transcendent "center" or "centers" that cannot be lost, but we have not tried to answer that question.

It may be important to separate the question of how a particular person puts his or her life together in terms of meaning and purpose (his or her "spirituality") and the question of the particular transcendent (or spiritual) values which are important to individual persons. We heard our interviewees talking about a number of values that they called "spiritual." We heard, for example, of the value of education. For some, this was the value of lifelong learning. For others, this was the value of education as it opened the door to opportunities for a "better life" for family members. In various ways, our interviewees reflected the traditional Chinese cultural emphasis on learning. We also heard about other values that the elders called "spiritual." We heard and observed the appreciation of art, particularly brush painting and calligraphy. We heard about music, dance, poetry, literature, and drama–both the classical and folk forms of these aspects of Chinese culture. We witnessed other kinds of esthetic forms in Taiwan and Singapore. We understood that these had "spiritual" value because they had lasting meaning and significance that spoke to individuals in different ways but transcended individual meanings. The value was expressed through particular forms but transcended those forms.

From some of our interviewees we heard about other kinds of values–what are often called "material" values. We heard about the importance for life now and for children and grandchildren in the future, of values such as a good job, earning enough money, having a good home, etc. We recognized the importance of such values in a culture with a rapidly rising standard of living, but we could not help but think about the transitoriness of such values. What kind of lasting meaning and purpose do such ''material'' values give to life? Does anyone ever have enough of such values? What happens if for some reason the material values are lost? Such questions are too simplistic, but they provide another perspective on the issues of ''self and world transcendence'' or the ''religious'' and ''spiritual issues'' that we have been discussing.

We also heard much about another value–health. From some perspectives and in some cultures, health might be considered as a ''material'' value–the way a person's body functions. But from other perspectives, including a ''holistic'' perspective, health includes not only how the body functions but how the whole person functions in his or her whole environment, particularly how the person ''puts it all together.'' Health is both a ''material'' and a ''spiritual'' value, both an individual value and a social value. The concern about health among the elderly is important and illustrates the complexity of the experience of aging and the interweaving of the various aspects of that experience.

CULTURE, RELIGION, AND SPIRITUALITY

In our preliminary outline of the interactions of personality and culture in the experience of aging we talked about the ways in which a particular culture:

> develops collective sources of meaning and purpose for life in which individuals can participate and which, to some extent, they can internalize through participation in myths, symbols, and rituals of the culture and/or some form of its religious heritage.

We are concerned about the impact of cultural change on traditional myths, symbols, and rituals of Chinese society as they affect the experience of the elderly in contemporary Taiwan and Singapore.

Some of our concern focuses, as we have noted, on definitions or images of "the good life" for the elderly. In Chapter Three we noted two kinds of image of "the good life" for elders in traditional Chinese society. The first and most common was the image of "long life" surrounded by children and grandchildren, enjoying a place of honor and respect in family and community, performing important roles and functions, and exercising authority in family and community. This is an idealized image, of course. It has some aspects of fantasy or "myth," but it also reflects important aspects of the actual place of elders in the traditional Chinese family.

The second image was Confucius' description of the ideal mature adult who at fifty knew "the biddings of heaven," at sixty "heard them with a docile ear," and at seventy "could follow the dictates of . . . (his) own heart, for what . . . (he) desired no longer overstepped the boundaries of right" (*Analects*, 2:4). This is the Confucian ideal of the internalization of ethical principles or values so that they become the "dictates of the heart." This ideal has been very important in the relations of family members with their elders in Chinese society. The primacy of family values over individual values, and the ethical principles of reciprocity, filial piety, and respect for elders have long been important for the relationships of family members to each other, particularly to their elderly members. One of the important issues from generation to generation has been the extent to which these values have been internalized by family members through the traditional processes of child rearing in family and community.

The Place of Family Rituals

Family rituals have played an important part in the processes of education in the family. The rituals associated with veneration of the ancestors (so-called "ancestor worship") have been an important part of family life, reminding all the family members of their ties to the older members of the family, both living and dead, and providing a place of honor in family celebrations throughout the year for the living elders and the dead ancestors. Rituals observing the birthdays and anniversaries of the death of departed elders have often been part of this process of remembering. Ideally, it was not only the departed elders who were remembered but also their contributions to the family, the ideals which they represented, and their place in the ongoing continuity of family life from generation to generation. Religious rituals have also served some of the same purposes and have provided social reinforcement of family values; but some Western religions, such as some forms of Christianity, have opposed rituals of ancestor veneration and have, in various ways, emphasized individual values rather than family values.

Internalization of Ethical Principles and Changing Images of "the Good Life"

Changes in familial and communal rituals sooner or later reflect changes in images of "the good life." We have noted some of the changes that have come with urbanization, industrialization, and modernization of life in Taiwan and Singapore. In Taiwan and Singapore, we observed increasing evidence of traditional familial and communal rituals being replaced by the rituals of a secular and materialistic society dominated by the popular media; but we also saw evidence of new images or "myths" of "the good life" for elders and new forms of ritual.

With the increasing fragmentation of family life and the weakening or breaking of the ties of continuity between the generations, images of the "good life" for elders have come to focus more on peer relationships. The development of peer groups of various kinds under both government and voluntary sponsorship is one aspect of this changing image. "The good life" in rural areas always involved important aspects of community life, and traditional religious institutions have also promoted forms of community. In the city and the suburbs, however, natural community tends to disappear and intentional forms of community life need to be developed. The activity centers in Taiwan and the community centers in Singapore, as well as the temples and churches, encourage increasing involvement in peer groups outside the family. The questions that we have raised about this aspect of "the good life" for elders have to do first with the extent to which this changing image of "the good life" is generally accepted by Chinese elders. And second, our questions have to do with what happens in the later phases or stages of the aging process when elders may no longer have the physical ability to participate in "long life clubs," activity centers, or religious groups. Our sense is that in Taiwan and Singapore, as in other parts of the world, images or "myths" of "the good life" for elders need to be developed which recognize the various stages of the aging process and include the infirm or "frail" elders as well as the more active ones. And for all Chinese elders, healthy as well as frail or infirm, our desire is for cultural images or myths of "the good life" that they can internalize throughout their life span and that can sustain them as spiritual "centers" of meaning and purpose for life in spite of the losses and insults that come with the aging process in the modern world.

The ways in which ethical values are internalized and contribute to the quality of life for the elderly are important not only for the elderly themselves; but in a family-oriented culture like the Chinese, they are also important for the relations between the generations. Confucius' concern for the internalization of ethical values takes on additional significance as we think about the future of the elderly in Chinese society. The question of the internalization of ethical values raises the question of the nature of the "spirituality" that will help the next generations to find meaning and purpose for their lives and will influence their relations with the elderly members of their own families. The question also focuses on the nature of the "center" or "centers" of the lives of the younger generation as they themselves grow old and on the processes by which meanings and values are internalized in an increasingly secular society that is dominated by the popular media. What will be the place of rituals and other traditional forms of familial and communal education in such a society?

Chapter Eight

Implications and Conclusions

We began this study with basic questions about what it means to be a person growing old in the context of Chinese culture. We knew something about Chinese culture from our previous experience in Singapore, our visit to Mainland China, contacts with Chinese students, and our continuing studies. We welcomed an opportunity to learn what we could about aging in the Chinese societies of Taiwan and Singapore. As we have reflected on the material that we have from our past and present studies, we have noted some implications that may be relevant for anyone concerned about the welfare of the elderly in those two parts of the world. More broadly, there are implications for those of us who are concerned about the welfare of the elderly in every part of the world.

In the previous chapter, we have shared some of our observations and thinking about the interactions of personality, culture, and religion in Chinese society in Taiwan and Singapore. There are two general implications that we want to discuss in this final chapter: the continuity and discontinuity of cultural patterns and values that influence the welfare of the elderly from one generation to another and the interactions of public and private social forces in promoting the welfare of the elderly. These are complex issues that need to be discussed at length. In this concluding portion of our study, we can do no more than highlight some of the reflections on these issues that have emerged from our study. We want to reflect on these issues from the perspective of some of the economic and political developments in the Chinese societies of Taiwan and Singapore.

1. CONTINUITY AND DISCONTINUITY
IN CULTURAL PATTERNS AND VALUES

The Singapore Committee on the Problems of the Aged was aware of this issue as it related to the welfare of the increasing numbers of elders in the next century. The report of the Committee, as we have seen, expressed concern about what kind of care persons born after 1947 will receive from their children when they retire. The trends which contribute to this concern are the decreasing number of children in Singaporean families, the changing lifestyles in which husbands and wives and their grown children work full time outside the home, and the signs of decline in filial piety and respect for elders. We have shared this concern in our own observations in the previous chapter.

The concern of the Singapore Committee reflects the wholeness of cultural patterns. Lin Yutang (1939) emphasizes how the whole of traditional Chinese society reflected the basic patterns and values of social behavior that were learned in the family. The family must interact with every aspect of the world around it, and major changes in that world inevitably affect the family. Similarly, major changes in family life affect the nature of society. The care of the elderly in Chinese society, as we have emphasized, is influenced by the traditional values of filial piety, reciprocity, and respect for elders. The world in which the younger generation is growing up is very different from the one in which their grandparents and parents were children.

The question of the transmission of cultural patterns and values is complex. What is happening to the family is basic, and we have noted some of the changes in the structure and styles of family living. The cohesive extended family that lived together under one roof and worked together on the family farm or in the family shop is rapidly disappearing. The nature of the family as an economic and social unit is changing. The kind of community in which most families live has changed radically. The impact of these changes on the family as a teacher of traditional cultural patterns and values is important; but many other changes are influencing the transmission of cultural values–changes in the goals and content of education, changes in the role and influence of religion, development of new and powerful forms of communication (radio, television, video, etc.) and, particularly, changes in the economic system and the social environment in which the family lives and works. Economic survival in today's world is no longer a family matter; it is a national concern which is being played out on a global stage. Nations like Taiwan and Singapore have learned much about economic survival and growth in a world in which their products must compete for markets all over the world. The impact on family life and every other aspect of culture is very great. These two nations have demonstrated remarkable ability to adapt to the demands of a global economy. Study of the welfare of the elderly highlights the importance of looking at the impact of economic and social changes on every aspect of culture and asking again the questions of what values the culture seeks to serve, what patterns of the traditional culture need to be preserved to serve those values, and how can the old and new patterns of life be reconciled with those values. Such questions need to be asked again and again in every part of the world as the rapid changes in the technologies of survival impact every nation and every person.

In this context, traditional values may need to be redefined in the light of changing situations. This is a complex process. An important part of this process should be careful reexamination of the meaning of traditional values. Filial piety, for example, when defined as absolute obedience to elders and rigid adherence to parental values may present serious problems in adjusting to a changing society. Reexaminations of the meaning of the filial piety, such as the one carried out by one of our doctoral students, become important (Yu, 1984). Historic or classical meanings then need to be examined in terms of the ethical situation in the contemporary family as it interacts with the modern world. Historic or traditional processes by which values have been transmitted from one generation to another also need to be examined in terms of their relevance in modern society, and attention needs to be given to how those processes can be preserved or new processes or modifications of the old ones can be developed in order to facilitate the internalization of values in each succeeding generation.

2. INTERACTIONS OF PUBLIC AND PRIVATE SOCIAL FORCES

The family-oriented values of Chinese society in Taiwan and Singapore make it possible to continue to emphasize the family as the primary source of care for the elderly. Our discussion of the continuity of cultural values has looked at the question of how long this emphasis can continue. Current policies and programs for the elderly and plans for the future reflect the view that the primary role of government is to enable elders to live with their families and to be supported by them as long as possible. Family care is to be supplemented primarily by private organizations and agencies under government supervision. However, the responsibilities of the government for destitute elders without families and for the elderly sick who cannot be cared for by families are recognized in both countries. Even in meeting these responsibilities, except for the care of veterans in Taiwan, the emphasis is primarily on government support and coordination of private agencies.

Our interviews in Taiwan and the data we had from Singapore provided evidence of how well this approach to the care of the elderly was working. Our discussion of our data, however, raised a number of questions about problems confronting a population with increasing numbers of persons in the sixty-five to one hundred (and over) age range. There are situations in which family resources may not be adequate. Our discussion of the continuity of cultural patterns and values highlighted some basic concerns.

A general concern is the importance of independent income for elders. Developing social insurance programs in Taiwan and the Central Provident Fund in Singapore respond to this concern, but our studies suggest that the need may be more extensive than current programs recognize.

There are other issues that we think need continuing attention. We can list some of these:

- the relations of nutrition and aging
- housing policies which encourage members of extended families living with or near each other
- standards of safe housing for elders

- transportation for frail elders at times when family transportation is not available
- development of nationwide health maintenance programs
- medical care for chronic and catastrophic illnesses
- resources to help families care for frail and infirm elderly
- problems of air and water pollution
- antismoking campaigns
- safety on the streets
- development of day care centers, home visitation, and telephone reassurance programs for the isolated elderly (with or without family)
- development of new forms of community life
- useful forms of work for elders outside the home
- education and recognition for volunteer activities of the elderly

We understand that steps have been taken in Taiwan and Singapore to meet some of these concerns since the time of our visits. Many of the concerns that have been listed can be met by the kind of government encouragement of private agencies that already exists, but public initiative in identifying needs and stimulating the development of private agencies will be important. Some of the concerns, however, require the attention of government agencies.

The efforts of the governments of Taiwan and Singapore to promote family and community initiative to meet the needs of the elderly are important. We were impressed with the ways in which the elders themselves were being encouraged to work together and to take responsibility for each other, in spite of some traditional Chinese attitudes toward strangers. There is a determination to find a Chinese way to respond to the problems of aging and to avoid the dangers of some Western "welfare state" approaches. The emerging Chinese model in these two countries deserves the attention of other countries that hold to the values of democratic institutions and private enterprise.

CONCLUSIONS

We began this study with our concern about the interactions of personality and culture, with a particular concern for the "religious" aspects of culture, although we have tried to redefine "religious" in the context of a "holistic" approach to the experience of aging.

The most obvious result of our study, for us, is that there are significant differences between the experience of aging in these Chinese societies and the experience of aging in white, middle class, American society. Aging in the two cultures is different for many reasons but primarily because the understanding and experience of family is different. Chinese elders, for the most part, prefer to live with their children, to keep the family as the primary focus of their social interaction, and to find much of the meaning of their lives and their hope for the future in their relationships with children and grandchildren. White, middle class, American elders prefer to live independently as long as possible, to enjoy their children and grandchildren from a distance (except for occasional visits), and to find the meaning and purpose of their lives and hopes for the future in their own personal interests and values (although there may be significant differences between men and women as to the extent to which these observations are appropriate). These are gross overgeneralizations, of course; but they represent outlines of basic cultural differences.

The data we have about the experience of Chinese elders in cities like Taichung, Taipei, and Singapore tell us about changes in family structures, relationships, and lifestyles. These changes have not yet altered the basic cultural orientation toward family among the elders with whom we talked and about whom we heard and read; but they are threatening to do so, and they have required that many elders find social relationships and sources of meaning and validation outside the family. But whether their relationships and sources of meaning and validation are inside or outside the family (or both), Chinese elders conduct their search in a Chinese way. For example, being a Chinese grandparent is different from being an American grandparent. Eating a meal with a Chinese family is a different kind of social experience than eating with a white, Anglo-Saxon Protestant family. Drinking tea with a group of Chinese men is a different experience from drinking coffee with a group of American men.

The interactions of personality and culture that we have observed mean, on the one hand, that being Chinese is different from being

American in both personal and social behavior and that the difference is partly the result of the differences between Chinese and American cultures; but, on the other hand, the interactions of personality and culture mean that there are very different ways of being Chinese just as there are different ways of being American. Those differences are at least partly the result of differences in individual personalities and individual life histories, as we have seen in Chapter Six. We met at least two Chinese elders whose reactions to their life experiences were highly individualistic. They had turned away from the family to follow personal interests and values. They seemed in some ways more American than Chinese. We learned of real differences between Mainlanders and native-born Taiwanese; between members of different economic and social classes; and between Christians, Buddhists, and "no religion" interviewees. And within these differences there were important individual variations.

We are impressed with the importance of the individual personality and the individual's ways of responding to his or her own experience of family and culture. We are also impressed with the "wholeness" of experience. We have used the separate categories of "physical survival," "social relationships" (socialization), "self-worth" or "place" (validation), and "sources of meaning and value" (self and world transcendence) to look at different aspects of the experience of aging. Our impression, however, from this and other studies of ethnicity and aging, is that these are not really separate categories. Each person brings together experience of these aspects of life into a whole that is his or her unique life.

The persons with whom we talked in Taiwan and most of the persons included in the Singapore Survey did not have major "physical survival" problems (income, housing, diet, transportation, medical care, etc.). The fact that they had reasonably good health meant that they could be physically active and enjoy social relationships with family and friends in a variety of settings. Major problems in any one of the areas of "physical survival" could have interfered, and sometimes had interfered, with their interactions with other persons and their place in life. We talked with elders who in the past had known real problems of income, family health, separation from family and/or homeland, or death of loved ones but had struggled hard and overcome these difficulties, usually for the sake of their families. We were interested in how these difficulties had affected other areas of their lives, and we were particularly interested in what they had learned out of their struggles. When we asked them what they learned from their hardships about what was important in life, we heard a variety of answers, depending on their religious commitments and their personal sense of values, but most of them had found something that made the struggle worth while.

It was our impression that most of the persons whom we had interviewed had experienced some kind of sense of personal worth or "place" in the eyes of their families that was supplemented for some by a sense of worth in their contribution to a community of persons (for example, church or activity center). They had also experienced a sense of meaning or purpose in something that transcended their day-to-day experiences–the meaning of family or art or social service or country or faith–something that transcended their own personal existence. These two different kinds of validation interacted with each other–their sense of worth or "place" in the eyes of others and their sense of meaning in their relationship to something greater than themselves.

A meaningful life for Chinese elders, as we observed it, involved all aspects of personhood. They were all important, and problems or deficiencies in any one aspect affected the others. The one exception was the commitment to a transcendent purpose (family, beauty, social welfare, country, God) that could make existence meaningful in spite of sufferings, deficits, and hardships in other aspects of life. Such commitment to a transcendent purpose we have discussed in terms of our interests in "religion" and "spirituality." We see such commitment as an important center around which to organize life and to find meaning and purpose for life in the face of the changing circumstances of the experience of aging. In this sense we think that every person is religious. Every person has some kind of "center," or possibly more than one "center," of value around which life is organized. We see religion in this sense as being particularly important for the later stages of the aging process when so many of the things that have given life meaning or purpose change or disappear.

The greatest concern arising out of our own interactions with Chinese elders is with those elders (of the present or succeeding generations) for whom family continues to be the primary source of meaning and purpose for life. What will life mean if the time comes that the ties with children or grandchildren are so altered by cultural change that they no longer have real significance, and there are no viable forms of community life to take their place? Elders may go on living on the dream that was part of their own heritage, but how long can they live on a dream that has less and less contact with reality? Much will depend upon the responses that individuals, families, and the Chinese societies of Taiwan and Singapore are making to the cultural changes that are now taking place.

As we bring this study to a close, we are grateful for the opportunity that we have had to gain some understanding of the many questions which have emerged and for this opportunity to make some contribution to the search for answers.

References

Buck, P.S. (1960). *My several worlds*. New York: Pocket Books (John Day, 1954).

Chang Ying-chang. (1984). *The problem of supporting the elderly in the changing family in Taiwan*. Paper presented to the 2nd Sino-American Conference on Social Welfare Development in the 1980s, August 12-15, 1984, San Jose, CA.

Chao Shou-Po. (1983). *The enhancement of the quality of life through community development in Taiwan, Republic of China*. Paper presented at the International Seminar on Community Development, May, 1983, Seoul, Korea.

Chao Shou-Po. (1984). *Family welfare in Taiwan, Republic of China–Its practice, problems, and future directions*. Paper presented to the 2nd Sino-American Conference on Social Welfare Development in the 1980s, August 12-15, 1984, San Jose, CA.

Confucius. (1938). *The analects of Confucius* (A. Waley Trans.). London: George Allen and Unwin.

Glasser, W. (1965). *Reality Therapy*. New York: Harper and Row.

Harris. L. & associates. (1975). *The myth and reality of aging in America*. Washington, D.C.: National Council on Aging.

Hsieh Jih-chang. (1984). *The quality of life for the elderly in a rural Taiwan village: The status of elderly fathers after family division*. Paper presented to the 2nd Sino-American Conference on Social Welfare Development in the 1980s, August 12-15, 1984, San Jose, CA.

Hsu, F.L.K. (1963). *Clan, caste, and club*. Princeton: Van Nostrand.

Ikels, C. (1983). *Aging and adaptation: Chinese in Hong Kong and the United States*. Hamden, CT: Archon Books (Shoe String Press).

Introduction to welfare for the aged in Taipei. (n.d.) Bureau of Social Affairs, Taipei City Government, Republic of China.

Jernigan, H.L. (1973). Some reflections on grief and mourning in Chinese society. *The South East Asia Journal of Theology, 18* (1), 21-47.

Jernigan, H.L. (1976). The Chinese clan as a caring community. *Pastoral Psychology, 25* (1), 5-15.

Jernigan, H.L. (1986). Some reflections on grief and mourning in Chinese society. in *Dealing with grief and loss*, Working Paper no. 1, Counseling and Care Centre, Singapore, 7-16.

Johnson, C. (1981). The Taiwan model. In Hsiung, J.C. et al. (Eds.). *The Taiwan experience.* New York: American Association for Asian Studies.

Labor standards law of the Republic of China. (1985). Ministry of Interior, Department of Labor, Republic of China.

Law of the aged peoples' welfare. (1983). Ministry of Interior, Republic of China.

Lee Kwan Yew. (1982). *The prime minister's Chinese New Year's message.* Press release, Information Division, Ministry of Culture, Republic of Singapore.

Lin Yutang. (1939). *My country and my people.* Bombay: Jaico Publishing House, 1960 (London: Heinemann, Ltd., 1939).

Maslow, A.H. (1968). *Toward a psychology of being* (2nd ed.). Princeton: Van Nostrand.

Myerhoff, B. (1978). *Number Our Days.* New York: Simon and Schuster.

Reid, D.P. (1984). *Taiwan.* Hong Kong: APA Productions; Englewood Cliffs: Prentice-Hall.

Report of the Committee on the Problems of the Aged. (1984). Singapore: Ministry of Health.

Report on the National Survey of Senior Citizens. (1983). Singapore: Ministry of Social Affairs.

Rogers, C.R. (1951). *Client-centered therapy.* Boston: Houghton Mifflin.

Rosow, I. (1965). And then we were old. *Transaction 2* (2), 20-26.

Singapore Facts and Pictures. (1984). Singapore: Information Division, Ministry of Culture.

Snygg, D. and Combs, A.W. (1949). *Individual behavior.* New York: Harper & Row.

Wee, Ann. (1983). *The dynamics of family life in Singapore, with special reference to the capacity of the family to provide care for the elderly.* Paper presented at the Asia-Oceania Regional Congress of the International Association of Gerontology, January, 1983, Singapore.

Wee, Ann. (1987). Personal correspondence.

Wolf, M. (1968). *The house of Lim: a study of a Chinese family.* New York: Appleton-Century-Crofts.

Wolf, M. (1972). *Women and the family in rural Taiwan.* Stanford: Stanford University Press.

Wong Mei-ching. (1982). Sociology of the aged: *An exploration into the social well-being of the Chinese aged in Chinatown.* Unpublished paper, Department of Sociology, National University of Singapore.

Wong, A.K. and Kuo, E.C.Y. (Eds.) (1979). *The contemporary family in Singapore.* Singapore: Singapore University Press.

Wong Chun-kit J. (1981). *The changing Chinese family in Taiwan.* Taipei: Southern Materials Center, Inc.

Yu Chi-ping. (1984). *Confucian and Biblical concepts of filial piety: Implications for pastoral care in the Chinese Church in Taiwan.* Unpublished doctoral dissertation, Boston University, Boston, MA.

APPENDIX A

Experts and Official Informants Interviewed in Taiwan and Singapore

The list is in the chronological order in which the interviews were scheduled.

TAIWAN

Mr. Han-hsien Ts'ai, Director, Bureau of Social Affairs, Taipei City Government

Dr. Li Chung Shu, Instructor, Department of Social Work, University of Chinese Culture, and Chief of Fourth Department, National Youth Commission (formerly Director of an Elder House)

Rev. John Lun Hsun Chang, S.J., Pastor, Holy Family Church, Taipei

Dr. Shou-Po Chao, Commissioner, Department of Social Affairs, Taiwan Provincial Government

Mr. Matthew Wang, Director, Populorum Progessio Institute, Taichung, and Director of a new activity center for elders

Mr. Lin Ter Feng, Social Worker with responsibility for elder affairs, Taichung

Miss Lo Yun Mei, Director, Taipei Evergreen Academy (activity center for elders)

Dr. Hsin-Huang Hsiao, Research Fellow, Institute of Ethnology, Academica Sinica, Taipei

Dr. Hou-sheng Chang, Professor, Department of Sociology, National Taiwan University

109

Mrs. Shu Jung Li, Social Worker, Assistant to the Director, Bureau of Social Affairs, Taipei

SINGAPORE

Dr. Gwee Ann Leng, M.D.

Dr. Gabriel C. Alvarez, Senior Lecturer, Department of Sociology, National University of Singapore

Dr. Stella R. Quah, Lecturer, Department of Sociology, National University of Singapore

Miss Florence Chan, Administrative Officer, Singapore Council of Social Service

Dr. Ann Wee, Director, Department of Social Work, National University of Singapore

APPENDIX B

Interviews with Elders:
Guidelines Provided to Students (1989)

INTERVIEW GUIDELINES
PASTORAL CARE AND CULTURAL PATTERNS: AGING

Purposes

1. The general purpose is to help the interviewer to develop insights into the experience of aging which will be helpful in present and future ministries with older persons.
2. The purpose of the interview with elders from a particular ethnic group is to develop a basis for comparison of the experiences of aging in different ethnic groups and to identify implications for present and future ministry with elders.
3. The specific purpose of the interviews is to establish relationships with older persons that help the interviewers to develop empathic understanding of their experiences of aging as well as insights into their situation as aging members of a particular ethnic group.
4. Past experience suggests that the interviews also serve as interesting and pleasurable contacts for the interviewees with students from the School of Theology.

Preparation

1. Study of the cultural background of the interviewees in relevant literature and discussion with at least one resource person who understands the culture.

111

2. Development of a holistic approach to the understanding of the experience of aging and an interview guide which reflects such an approach.
3. Familiarity with the interview guide and flexibility in achieving its purposes.
4. Developing the necessary contacts with interviewees.

Interview Format

Two interviews with each older person are recommended, if possible. The purpose of the first interview is to become acquainted with the interviewee(s) in his/her (their) life space. The second interview is to obtain information about various aspects of their experience of aging which were not included in the first interview. In both, factual data is important but not as important as the meanings and values which the interviewee(s) finds in various aspects of his/her (their) experience. The interviewer will need both data and intuitive and empathic impressions in order to reconstruct a ''picture'' of what it is like for each interviewee to be old in his/her particular situation.

INTERVIEW ONE

I. Introduction

The interviewer will need to introduce him/herself and state as clearly and simply as possible the purpose of the visit and answer any questions about what the interviewer will do with the information shared in the visit.

The general purpose of the first visit is to get acquainted with the interviewees and to give them a chance to share whatever they want to about themselves.

II. Body

If possible, follow the lead of the interviewee, asking questions to clarify what the interviewee is saying or to obtain related information. Empathic responses to the meanings or feeling expressed by the interviewee may help to encourage the interviewee to pursue important areas further.

Over the course of the two interviews it will be important to obtain information about the person and his/her situation, and some questions may be relevant during the first interview to supplement what the interviewee volunteers concerning him/herself and his/her situation. The interviewer will be trying to become acquainted with:

The person:

What does s/he want you to know about her/himself?
What is important to him/her?
How does s/he describe her/himself?
How does s/he feel about being old?

The living situation:

With whom does s/he live? How does s/he experience the relationship(s) with the other person(s)?
What about his/her personal living space? What are some of the important things (valuable to him/her) in that living space?
Are there any problems of comfort or safety?
How does s/he experience the neighborhood? Does s/he have a community?
Where does s/he go outside the house? How? What is it like?
What is his/her usual daily schedule? Weekly?
What does s/he enjoy most?
What about "special occasions?" What makes them special?
What are his/her interests and activities?
What does s/he worry about? What does s/he do about those worries?

The family situation:

Where do the members of his/her family live?
How often does s/he see them or have other contacts with them?

What is happening to the family now? What changes are taking place from generation to generation?
What does the family mean to him/her?

The cultural and religious situation:

How much contact does s/he have with people of similar age
and ethnic background? Where? When? What are the con-
tacts like?
How is his/her ethnic group changing? Why?
What are the traditional values of his/her ethnic group?
How does s/he feel about changes in values and lifestyle?
What is the place of the church, synagogue, or other religious
group in his/her life?
What does religion mean to her/him and what place does it
have in her/his life?

III. Conclusion

After a reasonable length of time (partly depending on the age
and strength of the interviewee), it will be important to bring the
first interview to a close, to express appreciation for the visit, and
to plan for a second visit, if possible.

INTERVIEW TWO

I. Introduction

A repeat introduction may be needed. The interviewee will need
to know that the interviewer may need to ask more questions to get
a more complete picture of what the interviewee has experienced.

II. Body

If possible, the interviewer should continue to emphasize listening and understanding but may need to ask questions in order to
have more comprehensive information about important aspects of

the interviewee's experience or to follow up leads from the previous interview. Probing for specific information concerning personal data is not advised. Accept what the interviewee is comfortable in sharing concerning the following aspects of experience. It is not important to have data concerning every item on the list. Note the information that is important to the interviewee.

a. Physical, survival aspects of experience:

   Safety
   Housing
   Nutrition
   Income
   Transportation
   Health care
   Sleep
   Exercise
   General physical condition

b. Socialization:

   Family relationships, past and present
   Peers
   Neighborhood
   Church and community
   Social networks and groups
   Shared interests and activities
   Emotional needs or problems

c. Validation:

   Sense of place in family, community, church, and world
   Role, function, status in family, community, church, and
      world
   Sense of self-esteem or self-worth
   Self-image, present and past

d. Self and world transcendence:

   What makes life worth living?

What has experience taught him/her?
What has been helpful in times of trouble? What is helpful now?
What would s/he want her/his children and grandchildren to learn?
What are his/her hopes for the future?
What are her/his hopes for children and grandchildren?

III. Conclusion

End the interview when a reasonable amount of time has been shared, even if all aspects of the interviewee's experience have not been covered. Do not make unrealistic promises about further contacts. End the interview in ways which are appropriate to the shared experience.

Index

Accidents, 43
Adoption, 25
Affection, 81
Aging
    conclusions on, 99-103
    and China-U.S. comparison,
        100-101
    and family structure, 22-25
    holistic approach to, 2-5
    *See also individual names and
        subjects*; Elderly
*Aging in Chinese Society: A Holistic
    Approach to the Experience
    of Aging in Taiwan and
    Singapore*, goals of, 7
Agriculture
    in Taiwan, 10-11
    and work force, 28-29
    See also Farms; Village life
Air pollution, 42
Alzheimer's disease, cost of, 37
Americans. *See* United States of
    America
Analects, 26
Ancestors
    family role of, 21-22,23
    and ritual, 91-92
Annual medical checkup, 78
Art, 58,83,89
    in case studies, 62,69-70
Atheists, 13
    in sample group, 5
    and self/world transcendence, 87
Attitudes, and filial piety, 35

Boston, Massachusetts, 1,27
Boston University, 6
British Commonwealth of Nations,
    16
British East India Company, 14
Brotherhood organizations, 25
Buck, Pearl, 23
Buddhists
    in sample group, 5
    and self/world transcendence, 87
Buddhism
    in case studies, 61,65
    in Taiwan, 12
Buses, 40
Bureau of Social Affairs, 62

Calligraphy, 58,62,69-70,83,89
Canada, 29,55,56,57,62,66
Cancer, 38
    See also Catastrophic illness
Cantonese, 15
Catastrophic illness, 41
    and family resources, 77
    and income, 37-38
    and government policy, 99
"Center"
    conclusions on, 102
    in spiritual life, 89
Central Provident Fund (CPF), 13,
    35-36,39,41,98
Chiang Kai-Shek, 10,11,12,65
    on village life, 52-53
Chinese, Singapore population of,
    15
Chinese society
    vs. American society, 100

117

and changing family, 96
family definition in, 20-22
family system in, 19-20
individual motivation in, 81
on respect, 81
See also Culture; Family system
Christianity, and individual values,
  92
Christians, 84
  in case studies, 61,68-69,70
  in sample group, 5
  and self/world transcendence, 87
  and socialization, 80
Churches and temples
  in case studies, 68
  and meaning of life, 57
  and peer-group involvement, 92
  questions about, 87
  and socialization, 45,47,48,80
  validation from, 82
Cities, 25-26
  and clan-substitute organizations,
    24
  and crime, 43
  and "good life," 92
  and socialization, 46,47-48,80
  validation factors in, 83
  See also Urbanization; Urban
    migration
Civil Code (Taiwan), 35
Clan, 22
  as family substitute, 24
Class, and philosophy of life, 55-56
Classroom for Mothers, 46
Climate, in Singapore, 13
Clothing, 74
Communication, changes in, 97
Confucianism, 50,75
  in case study, 68
  and ethical values, 93
  on family, 26
  and housing, 39
  on maturity stages, 91
  and social relationships, 20
  in Taiwan, 12,13

Confucianists
  in sample group, 5
  and self/world transcendence, 87
Coping pattern, 3
Creativity. *See* Art; Calligraphy;
    Drama; Music
Crime, 43
  See also Safety
Culture
  and China-U.S. comparison,
    100-101
  and education, 87
  in individual experience, 74
  and personality, 3-4
  in physical survival, 75-79
  in socialization, 79-81
  and societal changes, 96-97
  as transcendence factor, 85-88
  as validation factor, 81-85
  See also Chinese society

Data, role of, 4
Day care centers, 47,48
  and government, 99
Death, as validation factor, 83
Deceased, 23
  See also Ancestors
Depression, 42
  in case study, 65
Descendants
  family role of, 22
  See also Ancestors
Dialect
  impact of, 30,31-32
  and socialization, 47,81
Diet. *See* Nutrition
"Double nine days," 50
Drama, 58,89
Dutch explorers, 12

Economic system, changing nature
    of, 97
Economy, 15-16,37

Education, 83
  in case studies, 61,67-68,70
  and cultural changes, 96
  and morality, 50
  in Singapore, 16
  in spirituality, 89
  in Taiwan, 11
  as validation source, 83
Elderly
  case studies on, 59
  in cities, 25-26
  defined, 27
  family roles of, 20,22-24
  and government policy, 98-99
  outlook for, 100,103
  and physical survival, 34-43
  and self/world transcendence,
    85-88
  and socialization, 43-49
  and societal changes, 96-97
  and survival factors, 75-79
  and validation, 49-54,81-85
  without families, 24-25,26
  *See also individual names and
    subjects*
Elections, in Taiwan, 11
Electrification, 11
Employment, 36-37
English language, 6,32,81
  in Singapore, 15
  See also Dialect; Language
Environmental issues, 42
Ethical values
  and "good life," 92-93
  of young, 77
Evergreen Academies, 44,57-58
Exercise, 42-43,74
  extent of, 78-79
Extended family, 46
  and housing, 39
  in urban setting, 30

"Face," 3,20,49,74,82
Family
  in case studies, 60-71

  conclusions on, 103
  and cultural change, 96-97
  and income, 35-36
  increasing alienation from, 76
  and industrialization, 29-32
  meaning of, 20-22
  and philosophy of life, 55-57
  "place" in, 49
  and rituals, 91-92
  and socialization, 48-49,79-81
  societal impact of, 96
  substitutes for, 24-25
  and transportation, 40-41
Family planning, 51
Family shop, 29,76
  in case study, 65-68
  and family continuity, 56
Family system
  gender roles in, 19
  hierarchical structure of, 20
  See also Family
Farm life
  in case studies, 63-65
  and philosophy of life, 56
  See also Village life
Federation of Malaysia, 14
Filial piety, 39,50,77,80
  in case study, 66
  re-examination of, 97
First Opium War, 12
Flats, 39-40
  See also Housing
Food, 74
Friends, 45
  as validation factor, 83
Fukien province, 12

Generation gap, and urban living,
  31-32
Glasser, William, 3
"Good life," 26,91,92-93
Government, 16
  issues facing, 98-99
  primary role of, 98

Grandparents, 29,30
   case studies on, 61,62,63-64,65,
      66
   and family continuity, 56
   and quality of relationships, 80
   respect for, 82
"Granny suite" flats, 30,39

Hakkas, 11-12
Handicapped, 41,77
   in case study, 69,70
   and income, 83
Health, 37-38,74
   in case study, 64,69
   in holistic perspective, 90
   as validation factor, 84
   See also Catastrophic illness;
      Medical care
Health insurance, 41
Hokkein, 15
Holistic approach
   aspects of, 2-5
   health in, 90
   religion in, 73
Housing, 39,74
   in cities, 29,30
   and governmental policy, 98
   growing need for, 78
   and socialization, 46
Hsieh, Jih-chang, 45,48,52
Hsu, F.L.K., on clan, 22
Humanists, in sample group, 5

Ikels, C., 52
Immigration
   to Singapore, 29-30
   See also Mainlanders
Income, 74
   in case studies, 60-61,62,67
   and government, 98
   increasing importance of, 76
   and survival, 35-38
   in Taiwan, 11
   as validation factor, 84

Indians, in Singapore, 15
Individual, and family, 20-21
Individualism
   and Christianity, 92
   and motivation, 81
   trend towards, 77
Indonesia, 14
Industrialization, 1-2,6-7
   in Singapore, 29-32
   and socialization, 44
   in Taiwan, 10-11,28-29
Information, 3
Institutions, 3
Interpreter, 6
Interviews
   with farm families, 63-65
   limitations to, 6-7
   with "Mainlanders," 68-71
   role of, 5
   with shop owners, 65-68
   with urban migrants, 60-62

Japan, 12,14,62,65,67,80
Japanese, 15
Jernigan, Homer, 1,2
Jernigan, Margaret, 1,2
Johor, Sultan of, 14

Kai relationship, 25,45
Kampongs, 29
Kreta Ayer, 2
Kuan Kung, 13
Kuan Yin, 13

Language
   in case studies, 62,67-68
   as limitation, 6
   in Singapore, 15
   See also Dialect
Law of the Aged Peoples' Welfare,
      27,40
Lee Kwan Yew, 15

Life
  meaning and purpose of, 54-58
  See also Self transcendence
Life expectancy, outlook for, 28
Lin Yutang, 19
  on family system, 21
  on society-family relationship, 96
Literature, 58,89
Loneliness
  and case study, 70
  and support groups, 82
  and urban life, 48
Longevity, 49
  cultural role of, 23-24
  and income, 38
Long Life Clubs, 44,48,57-58,80
Love, 3,74
  importance of, 81

Mainlanders, 11
  in case studies, 68-71
  and elderly population, 28
  and philosophy of life, 55
Malay language, 15
Malays, in Singapore, 15
Malaysian Peninsula, 14
Mandarin, 6,12,15,32,81
Maslow, Abraham, 3
Massachusetts, 1,27
Materialism, growth of, 58
Meal delivery programs, 47
Meaning of life, 55-58,74
Media, 50
Medical care, 9
  and annual checkup, 78
  government role in, 98
  limitations to, 77-78
  See also Health
Men
  and employment, 37
  family role of, 19
  and longevity, 24
  number of, 5
  and retirement, 30-31
  and socialization, 46-47,48

  in village life, 52-53
  without family, 25
Middle class, and philosophy of life,
    55-56
Military pension, 36
Ming Dynasty, 12
Ministry of Community
    Development, 47
Ministry of Health, 2,34
Ministry of Social Affairs, 2,6,34
Missionaries, in Taiwan, 12,13
Modernization, 1-2
Moral education, in Taiwan, 17
Morality, and respect for elders, 50
Motivation, in socialization, 81
Mountains, in Taiwan, 10
Music, 58,62,89
My Country and My People (Lin),
    21
Myerhoff, Barbara, on working
    women, 37
Myth, 4,74
  and "good life," 93

Nationalist Chinese army, 10
Nationalist Survey of Senior
    Citizens, 6
National University (Singapore), 16
Natural resources, 3
Nature, and meaning of life, 58
"1982 New Year Address to the
    People of Singapore," 38,50
Nuclear family
  and housing, 39,46
  See also Family
Nutrition, 38-39,78
  and government policy, 98

Peer groups. *See* Support groups and
    peer groups
Pension, 36
  See also Retirement
Peoples' Action Party, 15

Peoples' Republic of China
  influence of, 36
  See also Mainlanders
Personal experience, basic aspects
    of, 3
Personality
  and China-U.S. comparison,
    100-101
  conclusions on, 101
  in physical survival, 75-79
  in socialization, 80-81
  as transcendence factor, 85-88
  as validation factor, 83-84
Phenomenological approach, 4
Philippines, 10,14
Philosophy of life, 85-88
  See also Religion; Self
    transcendence
Physical survival
  conclusions on, 101-102
  defined, 3
  and exercise, 42-43
  and housing, 39-40
  factors in, 74,75-79
  and income, 35-38
  and medical care, 41-42
  and nutrition, 38-39
  and safety, 43
  and sleep, 42,43
  and transportation, 40-41
Physical therapy, 78
"Place," 74,85
  conclusions on, 102
  factors in, 52
  in family, 49-52
Poetry, 58
Poor, housing for, 39
Populorum Progressio Institute, 48
Press, on morality, 50
Pride, 82
Provincial Department of Social
    Affairs, 42
Provincial Government, 11
Purpose of life, 55-58,74

Radio, 31,45
Raffles, Sir Stamford, 14
Reading, role of, 4-5
Recession, 37
Reciprocity, and family substitutes,
    25
Religion, 4,5
  in case studies, 68-69,70
  changing nature, 96-97
  conclusions on, 102
  etymology of, 8
  and hard times, 75-76
  in holistic approach, 73
  in individual experience, 74
  in physical survival, 75-76
  and ritual, 91-92
  in socialization, 80-81
  in Taiwan, 12-13
  as transcendence factor, 87,89-90
  as validation factor, 83-84
Remarriage, 48-49
*Report of the Committee on the
    Problems of the Aged,* 2,6-7,
    34,35,39,45,48
  on exercise, 42-43
  main concerns of, 96
  on morality, 50-51
  on socialization, 47
*Report on the National Survey of
    Senior Citizens,* 2,34
  on family decline, 79-80
Republic of China. *See* Taiwan
Respect for elders, 22-23
  in case study, 61
  decrease in, 82
  importance of, 81-82
  and modernization, 49-52
  and urban living, 31
Retirement, 36
  age of, 27
  and income, 37-38
  and self worth, 54
  and socialization, 45,48
  and urban life, 30-31
  and village life, 52-53

Rice, 10
Ritual, 4,74
  in family life, 91-92
Rogers, Carl, 3
Rosow, I., 52
Rural areas. *See* Farm life; Village
  life

Safety, 43
  government standards for, 98
  responsibility for, 78
Sample group
  makeup of, 5
  size of, 2
Sanitation, 74
Second Opium War, 13
Self, defined, 3
Self-esteem, 3,74
Self trancendence, 55-58,74
  conclusions on, 102
  remaining questions on, 85-88
  and spirituality, 88-90
Senior citizens. *See* Aging; Elderly
Senior Citizen's Club, 45-46
Senior Citizens Health Centers, 41
Shame, 82
Shop. *See* Family shop
Singapore
  change and modernization in, 27,
    30-32,33-58
  data and background on, 13-17
  dialect in, 30,31-32
  "elderly" defined in, 27
  elderly population in, 27-28
  government concerns in, 98-99
  impact of change in, 96-97
  interest in, 1-2
  outlook for, 100
  research sources in, 2
  retirement age in, 27
  socialization factors in, 79-81
  study limitations in, 6-7
  survival factors in, 75-79
  validation factors in, 81-85

*See also individual names and
  subjects*
Singapore Fact and Pictures, 1984,
    13,17
Sleep, 42,43,74,78
Smoking, 42,99
Socialization, 4,74
  factors in, 43-49,79-81
Social welfare, 57,80,85
  in case study, 62
Spain, 12
Spirituality
  conclusions on, 102
  role of, 89
  See also Religion
Standard of living
  and income, 35
  and material values, 89-90
  and physical survival, 77
  in Taiwan, 11
Status, in peer groups, 82
"Stem" family, 46
Strangers, 47-48
Suburbs
  in case study, 63,64,69
  and "good life," 92
Subway, 40
Suez Canal, 14
Sun Yat Sen, 87
Support groups and peer groups
  and "Good life," 92
  non-family, 24-25
  and philosophy of life, 57-58
  and socialization, 40-49,80
  validation from, 82-83
Surname associations, 25,26
"Survivors," 49
Symbols, 4,74
Systems, 3

Taichung, 48,100
Taipei, 29,40,62,100
Taiwan
  aging population in, 27,28

change and modernization in,
  28-32,53-58,97
data and background on, 9-13
"elderly" defined, 27
family in, 21
and future, 57
government concerns in, 98-99
interest in, 1-2
language in, 31-32
research sources on, 2
survival factors in, 75-81
study limitations in, 6-7
validation factors in, 81-85
*See also individual names and
  subjects*
Taiwanese, and philosophy of life,
  55
Taiwanese language, 6
See also Dialect; Language
Tamil, 15
Taxis, 40
Tea drinking, 100
  in case study, 61
  and socialization, 46-47
  social meaning of, 58
Technology, 3,6-7
  and family alienation, 76
  impact of, 31
Telephone, 30,31
  in case study, 60,70
Television, 31,45
Teochow, 15
Tools, 3
Tourism, in Singapore, 15
Transportation, 11,40-41,74
  in case study, 60
  government role in, 9
  and socialization, 83

United States of America, 55,56,57,
  66,67,70
  aging population in, 27-28
  compared to China, 100
  and urban crime, 43

Urbanization, 1-2,6-7
  in Singapore, 29-32
  and socialization, 44
  in Taiwan, 28-29
  See also Cities; Urban migration
Urban migration
  in case studies, 60-61,64
  and family "place," 53-54

Validation
  defined, 3
  and family "place," 49-52
  interacting factors in, 81-85
  in village life, 52-54
Values
  changing nature of, 96-97
  family vs. individual, 92
  and filial piety, 35
  material, 89-90
  in validation process, 84
Vandalism, 43
Veterans, 36
Video cassette recorders, 31
Village life
  and elder "place," 52-53
  and "good life," 92
  and validation, 83
  See also Farm life
"Void deck" groups, 44-45,47
Volunteerism, 48,57-58,80
  in case studies, 68

Water, cleanliness of, 42
Weather, 80
Wee, Dr. Ann, 25
Westernization
  and welfare state, 99
  of young, 77
Whiting Foundation, 1
Widow, 24
Wolf, Margery, 2,45
  on family, 21
  on village life, 53

on working women, 37
Women
  and employment, 37
  family roles of, 19
  and longevity, 24
  number of, 5
  and retirement, 30-31
  and socialization, 46-47,48
  in village life, 52,53
  unmarried, 24-25
Work
  and government policy, 99

See also Retirement
Working class, and philosophy of
  life, 56
World transcendence, 55-58,74,
  88-90
  conclusions on, 102
  defined, 3
  remaining questions on, 85-88

YMCA, 68
Young
  family roles of, 23
  Westernization of, 77